About the Author

Kate Pleace is a senior women's health nurse and nurse lecturer, specialising in fertility, POI and menopause.

Progesterone and Me

Kate Pleace

Progesterone and Me

Olympia Publishers
London

A CIP catalogue record for this title is
available from the British Library.

ISBN 978-1-83543-355-3

First Published in 2025

Olympia Publishers
Tallis House
2 Tallis Street
London
EC4Y 0AB
Printed in Great Britain

Dedication

This book is dedicated to my husband, Dave, who was there with me throughout the journey that not only changed us but also opened up a new future.

Acknowledgements

To my husband, the love of my life, who was always there. To my mum and sister Claire, my sister-in-law Tracy who took amazing photos of us as well as Dave's family. To my work wife Jackie and my close friends, Holly, Kerry, Anne, Lian and Clare who listened to or brought chocolate. A big thank you to my Bourn Hall family who never stopped believing. To my four-legged family, the Pleace Pack, Lottie, Ralph, Margi, and Titch who were always there for a dog snuggle or a walk along the beach to clear my head when the brain cells stopped working! To my fertility and menopause nurse buddies: Tori, Donna, Julie, Kate and Andreia; wonderful supportive friends and colleagues who are experts in women's health. Your knowledge and support were vital in helping me take the big writing step! To the Centre of Reproduction Research, who believed in me and provided the opportunity to pursue a PhD in POI. Finally, all the men and women who, like me, found an alternative ending after unsuccessful fertility treatment.

Introduction

D-Day

It was a Tuesday morning in May 2017, a couple of months after it had all happened. After yet another sleepless night, I was truly at rock bottom. This had been going on for months, me in tears and hysterics, and I was now starting to climb the walls. I wanted it to end right there and then; this was no life, and I wanted it all to go away. I looked up at my husband, Dave, who had his head in his hands, softly saying, 'I just don't know what to do any more.'

As I shuffled into the doctor's surgery, still crying, a thought entered my mind: How had I gotten here? Just a few months ago, in January, I was a hardworking fertility nurse with a love of running and cookies. Now, as I walked through the consultation door with my husband, I could barely stand. The physical symptoms had improved somewhat, but the psychological symptoms, including depression, flashbacks, insomnia, and severe anxiety, were worse, almost non-stop. The GP looked at me in shock, and while she was lovely, I didn't expect her to have a cure or an answer, but she was kind and took the time to listen. She also prescribed me some new medication, which meant I didn't have to try the sleeping pills again. I didn't expect these pills to do much; after all, look what had happened when I tried other medications. However, they gave me the first few hours of sleep in months, the one thing I needed to break the cycle. But where did it all start?

Chapter 1

When the Two Merge,
the Nurse Becomes the Patient

I didn't become a nurse until I was in my late 20s. Many people say they knew nursing was for them and it was all they wanted to do. For me, I wasn't so sure. I knew I wanted to do something that made a difference and helped others. When I was 18, I thought I wanted to be a midwife. I applied to university while still at school but didn't get the grades needed to get onto the course. At the time, I was devastated. Things always seem intense when you're young, but looking back, it was probably a blessing. I was just 18, and being a midwife is a very responsible role. I have no doubt that at such a young age, I would not have been ready for it. It gave me time to grow up, live in the world and gain some life experience. I found a job in a bank and then worked in admin for a few years before I began to rethink what I wanted to do.

It came back to wanting to make a difference. I liked working in administration, but it felt as if when I wasn't at work, nobody would notice. That's when I began to explore other options and decided I wanted to become a nurse. Even before I started the course, I knew I wanted to work in the area of women's health. Women make up 51% of the population, yet we don't always receive the care and support we need. I found this area fascinating; it sparked a passion in me and I couldn't wait to get started, focusing my final management placement on gynaecology.

Nurse training, when I started back in 2004, lasted three years and consisted of clinical placements and university lectures. Once I qualified as a general nurse (RN), I worked on a busy gynaecology ward for a number of years. This provided me with valuable experience in acute care within a specialist area, and I was also able to work in early pregnancy and gynaecology outpatients. Nursing is highly portable and valued, so I spent a year living and working in Australia, nursing in Sydney and Queensland. When I returned to the UK, I saw a job opening for a fertility nurse which made me remember a television programme I had watched years earlier about a couple undergoing IVF. This must have been in the early days of IVF in the mid-90s, as I was a teenager at that time. I remembered how fascinated I was by the process, the pictures of eggs and embryos and thought, *Wow, this is an area I would love to work in and learn more about.* This gave me the confidence to apply for a role in this new and exciting area, and I managed to get an interview.

I was lucky to be offered my first post in fertility nursing. I remember when they phoned the following day to offer the job, I was so surprised and said, 'Have you got the right person?' I was keen to start learning and experiencing this new speciality. Fertility nursing is quite different from gynaecology. Looking back, I would compare that first year to being in a spin dryer on a backward cycle.

"Everything you already know is relevant, but the bigger picture just doesn't quite seem to make sense." Luckily, with time, experience and mentorship from colleagues, combined with a lot of reading, I began to feel much more confident in the role after about a year.

It's a role like no other. Your patients are predominantly fit and well but still need your help and support. The one thing they have always wanted is often out of their reach – a baby, a family. As a fertility nurse, a key part of this role is supporting patients. It can be a double-edged sword: some days are very positive when treatment works or a patient brings in their baby. Other days are extremely challenging when you are often breaking bad news or supporting patients when their treatment sadly hasn't worked.

Working in the area of fertility offers many opportunities for nurses. We are there for the patient from the start to the end of their journey and get to work with an amazing multidisciplinary team of doctors, administrators, embryologists and counsellors. We all play an integral part of the team. There are also many advanced roles that nurses can take on, and I relished the opportunity. I took on extended roles, learning to perform pelvic ultrasound, take blood, provide patient sedation and also undertook the role with a cherished friend and colleague, running a multi-site egg donation programme. There was also an opportunity to go to different conferences which was a real treat particularly for a nurse, as we don't always get to go to the conferences. I was able to go to fertility conferences in Dublin, Glasgow, Brighton, Leeds, Helsinki Belfast, and Edinburgh over the years.

Fertility Fact

What Does a Fertility Nurse Do?

If you are having fertility treatment, there is a team of health care professionals who will look after you during your treatment. This team may include doctors, embryologists, nurses, administrators and counsellors. Nurses are the key part of the team who take care of you. They are usually there from the start to the finish of your treatment. They may be there at your consultation helping you complete the consent forms or taking your blood for testing. They usually have an appointment with you to explain your treatment cycle and since many of the medications are self-injected at home, they will usually teach you how to do your injections or any other medications and help you write your treatment schedule and instructions.

Once your treatment starts, your fertility nurse becomes a key part of it. They would be teaching you how to self-inject your medication, doing your treatment scans or assisting with other procedures such as egg collection or embryo transfer. They support you all the way, answering any questions, offering a kind listening ear or telling you what to expect next. After you have had your treatment, whatever the outcome is, it is likely that they will be the first people you talk to at the clinic. If your treatment goes well, they might be doing your pregnancy scan, and if the treatment isn't successful, they might be chatting to you on the phone providing you the vital support you need the most.

It's a varied and responsible role that many nurses enjoy. There is variety as they work in different areas from theatre and clinic to recovery and administration. You can also have the opportunity to learn advanced skills such as pelvic scanning and specific fertility procedures. If you wish, you can also specialise further within different areas, such as focusing on egg donation or surrogacy. There is also an opportunity to attend different conferences and study days to share knowledge and advance your practice.

People would often say to me, 'Wow, that must be such an enjoyable role, every day must be a celebration for you and your patients.' But the truth is, yes, while some days are indeed a celebration when treatment goes well or patients bring in their baby to meet you, other days can be the complete opposite as it might be breaking bad news due to nonviable pregnancy scans or treatment that hasn't gone as expected or be speaking to patients who have had a negative pregnancy test and need your support. You develop key skills and get support from the nurses in the team and the staff at the clinic so that you can cope on the days which are not a celebration but important and likely to impact both you and the lives of your patients.

I had been working in the area of fertility for three years when Dave and I decided to try for a baby, even though I knew that it would be a challenge, as I was aware that I had very irregular periods. I never thought that I would walk on the same path as my patients. I remember when our NHS referral was sent, I said to my husband, crying, 'I never thought we would walk this path.'

Chapter 2

Fertility Journey

It all begins with the egg.

As women, we are born with all the eggs we will ever have and at birth, the estimate is that a baby girl is born with around 1–2 million eggs. Did you know that your grandmother carried part of you? This is because a female foetus is born with all the eggs she will have in her lifetime and when your grandmother was pregnant with your mother, you were a tiny egg in one of her ovaries, so the three of you have been connected for a long time – how amazing is that?

Once a baby girl is born, the number of eggs begin to decrease, and by the time the baby girl reaches puberty, the number is on average i.e., around 300,000, which is around 25% of the remaining ovarian reserve. Once a woman reaches her thirties, this number reduces to around 120,000. By late thirties, the number dramatically declines to around 25,000, and by the time a woman is in her fifties and has reached menopause, this number is thought to be around only a 1000. A woman is not able to make any more eggs after she is born. It is important to know that the number of eggs we are born with can be individual to us as women, so you may not be born with the same number of eggs as your sister or friends.

The eggs in the ovary, also known as oocytes, are immature or primordial and stay suspended from birth until puberty. The eggs are stored within the follicles in the ovaries. The human egg is the largest cell in the body. If you take a sharp pencil and make a tiny dot on a piece of paper, then that would be around the size of a human egg. Once puberty starts and the menstrual cycle begins, the eggs grow and mature every month during a cycle. As a young girl, when we first start our periods, normally, they may be irregular, heavy and unpredictable. Research suggests that it takes around six years for the menstrual cycle to normalise. However, if you notice anything about your periods that worries you such as extreme bleeding or pain, it is important to discuss this with your healthcare professional who can advise you further.

During each menstrual cycle, a pool of follicles is selected, recruited and begin the maturation process; however, it is normal that many of the eggs do not reach maturity and will usually die off before ovulation, a process known as atresia. This is what accounts for the loss of so many eggs over a woman's lifetime. Usually around the time of ovulation, one dominant follicle is selected that is large enough for ovulation when the mature egg is released.

The menstrual cycle is divided into phases which includes the follicular phase, that starts with your periods and it is when the egg begins to grow and develop. Next phase is the ovulation phase, which is when the egg is released and final phase is the luteal phase, where hormone levels will decrease if the egg hasn't been fertilised. There are four major hormones responsible for regulating the menstrual cycle. Follicle stimulation hormone (FSH) and luteinizing hormone (LH) are produced in the pituitary gland in the brain. The ovaries produce oestrogen and progesterone during the menstrual cycle. This means, your brain and reproductive system are working together throughout the cycle to ensure the hormones are released at the right time to support the growth of the egg.

Let's take a closer look at the three phases of the menstrual cycle. The cycle begins with the ovulatory phase. Two hormones from your brain FSH and LH begin to stimulate the growth of a small pool of eggs in the ovaries. These hormones also trigger the production of oestrogen. As the level of oestrogen begins to rise, think of the oestrogen as a switch which then turns off the production of FSH. This careful hormone balance allows the body to limit the number of eggs that continue to develop and mature. The ovulatory phase usually starts around the middle of a woman's cycle. As the hormone oestrogen begins to rise and the follicle is approaching ovulation, the follicle triggers a surge in LH which causes the dominant follicle to release the egg.

Once the egg is released, it travels through the fallopian tube towards the uterus. During this time, the egg is capable of being fertilised for a short number of hours. If the egg is not fertilised during this window, it will wither and die. The luteal phase can last around 10–15 days, and the empty follicle develops a new structure known as a corpus luteum, which then secretes the hormone progesterone. Progesterone prepares the uterus for a fertilized egg to implant and to support a potential pregnancy. If the egg isn't fertilised, progesterone levels begin to fall and the lining of the uterus breaks down resulting in a period. The cycle then begins again.

On average, a typical menstrual cycle lasts around 28 days. However, every woman is individual and unique, and some women may have a shorter cycle, typically less than 25 days, or a longer cycle which may be up to 35 days. Recent evidence suggests that menstrual cycle is the key indicator of your overall health. Therefore, it is important to monitor your cycle so that you can find out what is normal for you and then if you experience any change in your cycle such as irregular periods, heavy periods or absent periods, you can discuss these changes with your health care professional.

The menstrual cycle continues throughout a woman's life until most of the eggs in the ovaries are depleted. This is known as menopause. The average age of menopause in the UK and Europe is around 50–52. The menopause only refers to one day in a woman's reproductive cycle, which is 12 months after her last period. However, hormones can begin to change many years or months before a woman's last period. This period is known as the perimenopause or menopause transition. Often during this time, periods can change, becoming closer together, further apart, heavier or lighter. We refer to the time after the menopause as postmenopausal. A woman is postmenopausal the day after menopause and will remain so for the rest of her life.

"It's me, Hi, I'm the Problem" Taylor Swift. *Anti Hero* (2022)

I had never wanted children until I met my second husband, Dave. I can't explain it, but after we had been together for a few months, it all seemed possible with the right person. I always suspected that it would be challenging to try to conceive because I knew my cycles before being on long-term contraception which stopped my periods that were unpredictable and irregular. But we could never imagine what lay in store for us or the path that lies ahead. Initially, like many other couples, we began trying naturally but ran into a problem straight away after I had my Mirena coil removed. My periods changed and were still unpredictable but now extremely irregular either with episodes of prolonged bleeding or months without a period which made it extremely difficult to try to conceive naturally.

I eventually went to see my GP which is what I advise most patients to do. He was aware that I worked in the area of fertility and referred us to our local fertility clinic. In 2013, there wasn't a long waiting list to see our local NHS fertility clinic like there is now and we were luckily seen within a few months, which is much different from the patients I see now who are likely to be waiting for many months to see their NHS fertility clinic because of increased waiting times and pressures on NHS. We had all the initial blood tests and pre-work-up tests done which included an ultrasound and tubal patency test. It was then while listening to the sonographer writing up the scan report that I realised things would be even more difficult, my ears went up when they heard a low antra follicle count. It was me, I was the problem! I knew from all the years being a fertility nurse that this would mean I might have a low ovarian reserve and may need more help to potentially get pregnant.

My tubal patency test and Dave's semen assessment results were both normal, so we tried two rounds of ovulation induction. (You can find out more about that in the fertility ladder of treatment.) I didn't respond on either cycle. We then came back to see the consultant who then referred us to IVF. We were very lucky that we were eligible for NHS funding. This can vary depending on where you live in the UK and your circumstances. Different things that can impact your eligibility include your age, BMI, if you smoke and if you have had children from another relationship. Different areas have different criteria which can also change over time, and this is often referred to as a postcode lottery.

For many patients referred for IVF on the NHS, this means that they may have to access a different fertility clinic known as a tertiary clinic. This is because there are only a few NHS fertility clinics that offer IVF. The majority of clinics are private fertility clinics that have a contract with the NHS to deliver IVF for their patients. I knew that I would have the choice of two different clinics based on where we lived; one was the clinic I worked in and the other was based in London. Different clinics may have the NHS contract in your area, so it is always a good idea to ask this question if your NHS consultant is looking to refer you for NHS IVF treatment. I chose to have treatment in the clinic I worked in. I knew this would be a hard choice for us and my work colleagues, but it was the right decision for us. This was based on several factors. We trusted everyone at my clinic implicitly and felt comfortable with people we knew. We were restricted to this choice also because we were NHS funded, we could only choose the clinic I worked in or a clinic that was further away. A clinic that was further away would mean more problems on a practical level for us both including travel time and navigating the journey around our work commitments.

It made sense to think about the practicalities; I didn't want our fertility journey to eat up into our work and felt more comfortable if we could travel less. Dave also worked a short distance from the clinic , so he would be nearby if needed. I often talk to my patients at length about the practicalities when deciding to choose a fertility clinic. This can be just as important as clinic success rates as you may have to visit the clinic several times during the treatment. Taking in all the possibilities, it was the right decision for us and my lovely colleagues at my clinic looked after us with grace and were there for us at all the stages of the rollercoaster that is IVF. We tried two cycles of IVF using my eggs in 2014 and 2015, and the blood test which were taken earlier showed that I had a low ovarian reserve and may not respond to the treatment.

Fertility Fact

What Is a Low Ovarian Reserve?

Think back to earlier when I talked about women having a

reserve of eggs. As women, we all have our ovarian reserve. This is what we are born with as a baby, and it slowly reduces with time. Ovarian reserve is important because once our egg supply starts to run low, this can make getting pregnant more challenging. Think of your ovarian reserve as a jar of Smarties. It starts off full but then reduces over time. If you eat the Smarties, there are fewer in the jar and the ones at the bottom may not be as nice as the ones on the top of the jar. Just like the jar of Smarties, our egg quantity and quality reduce as we age; however, some women may be born with fewer eggs – less Smarties in the jar – and some women may lose more eggs as they age – losing more Smarties from the jar.

Most fertility clinics use an Anti-Mullerian Hormone blood test known as an AMH blood test. AMH is the hormone that the small follicles not being used in a cycle within your ovaries produce. This is usually taken as part of your pre-treatment tests. This is a blood test that comes back with a number that gives the clinician an idea of what your ovarian reserve is. The higher the number the better the ovarian reserve. It is important to note that if we are born with ovaries, we may all have a different number if the test was taken which is normal for us. There isn't much that can be done to change this number; however, the result will give the clinician an idea of how you may respond to fertility treatment and what treatment and protocol may be right for you.

A low AMH result can indicate a low ovarian reserve. This is because the test measures the anti-mullerian hormone which is a hormone the small follicles in your ovaries produce. If your ovarian reserve is lower, you produce less of this hormone. Being told you have a low ovarian reserve can be a shock and have a big impact on what fertility treatment you may decide to have. It is important to keep this in perspective as a low ovarian reserve does not mean that a pregnancy is impossible or that you may be approaching menopause. We know of women having fertility treatment who have had a low ovarian reserve and still had a successful treatment and who had both a pregnancy as well as a baby.

We do not routinely test most women's ovarian reserve or AMH level. It tends to be used only if you consider having fertility treatment. Therefore, there may be women who have never had any fertility treatment who may still have a low AMH and would not be aware of this and who may have also conceived a pregnancy naturally. We also don't know the path each woman takes with their AMH level, as it can change over time. We know as we age, it reduces. However, there is no set path as we are all individuals. Most clinics will also not just base your treatment options on your AMH result, they will look at the complete picture including an ultrasound scan, if applicable your partner's semen assessment, other blood tests and your medical history.

My AMH was less than 3, so this was on the low side for my age. Again, this number can be very individual for each person, but it was clear that overall this was low and would likely impact our chances of success. We also know that some women with a low AMH are likely to need higher dosages of IVF medication to achieve an optimum response and that women with a lower AMH may produce fewer eggs at egg collection than women with an AMH in the normal range.

The first IVF cycle for us was positive. I responded to the treatment which was a good start, as I feared I may not, and four of my eggs were collected with two embryos transferred. By the day after our egg collection, when the lovely embryology team called us for our first check, the number was down to 2 embryos. However, whilst these embryos were suitable for transfer, they were both not of a high grade, so I knew the chances of it working were low. We then had both embryos transferred two days after our egg collection, known as a day 2 transfer.

Fertility Fact
The Embryo's Journey

After eggs and sperm have been collected, the embryologist will put eggs and sperm together in one of two ways, conventional IVF, where eggs and sperm are placed in a dish and media, and allowed to fertilise naturally or ICSI, where each egg is injected with a sperm, and fertilised. The eggs are then placed in a dish with special media and allowed time to see if they fertilise. The embryologists check on them the following day to see if any of the eggs have fertilised and have formed embryos. They then monitor and grade the embryos deciding on the best day for an embryo to be replaced, known as an embryo transfer.

The embryo has a predictable journey over the next few days if it is developing normally, certain cell stages are expected to be seen when the embryologists observe the embryo down the microscope.

Day 1 – Looking for fertilisation
The eggs are checked to see if they have fertilised. The fusion combining of the egg and sperm, a normal fertilisation is the presence of two pronuclei, one from the egg and one from the sperm.

Day 2 – Checking for cell division
The embryos are checked once again to assess cell division, at this point most embryos will have 2–4 cells. If the embryo has not been divided by this time, it is sadly considered to be non-viable.

Day 2/3 – Possible transfer day

By day 3, embryos usually have 6–8 cells and the embryologists may decide this day to be the best day to have the embryos transferred, day 2 is the earliest day an embryo can be transferred back to the uterus.

Day 4 – Compacting

The embryos continue to grow and develop into a compact ball of cells which is called a morula. At this time, it is no longer possible to count the cells in the embryo.

Day 5 – Forming a blastocyst

By day 5, the embryo has been developed into a blastocyst. At this stage, it is possible to see two structures, the inner cell mass, which will go on to form the baby, and the trophectoderm cells which go on to form the placenta. Blastocysts can also be graded to assess the best embryo for transfer.

Day 6 – Final day to transfer or freeze embryos

This is the last day an embryo can be transferred or frozen.

It is important to be aware that every clinic can be different and there will be variations in the protocols and grading systems each clinic uses, so it is always good to speak to your embryologist about this either beforehand or when they call you to give you an update on your embryos. Your embryologist is highly knowledgeable and happy to answer your questions during your treatment cycle.

Fertility 101

Your embryologist might just be your first babysitter!

Jokes aside, your embryologist has a very important job,

they look after your gametes (eggs, sperm and embryos) put them together and then look after and monitor your embryos until it is time to have an embryo or embryos transferred back to your uterus. Embryologists are also responsible for freezing and storing any gametes for future treatment.

Embryologists are highly skilled and trained individuals who work in the laboratory undertaking all the lab work that is required for your IVF cycle. They complete years of training and competencies to be able to do this varied and important job. They also use a variety of high-tech equipment to monitor your embryos along the way.

You never know as the human body can always do things that surprise you, but sadly, cycle 1 ended in a negative pregnancy test. We tried again with cycle 2 a few months later, but this also did not go so well, and I did not respond to the stimulation treatment at all. Sadly, this cycle was cancelled before getting to egg collection. This was a devastating decision because I knew in my heart that it was over for any treatment with my eggs. I remember sitting in the nurse's office, crying after I had phoned Dave at home and told him about the news. After my scan, it felt like a part of our journey was over. After many months of tests and two cycles of failed IVF treatment using my eggs at the age of 34, I was diagnosed with premature ovarian insufficiency.

Premature ovarian insufficiency is a menopause before the age of 40. This is a rare condition with around 1 in 100 women under the age of 40, 1 in 1000 under the age of 30 and 1 in 10,000 under the age of 20. There are a variety of reasons why a woman may experience menopause before the age of 40. This can include a family history of premature menopause, genetic reasons, infection, surgery or other medical conditions. However, for the majority of women, often the cause is idiopathic, meaning the cause is sporadic or unknown. After this diagnosis, I was in a bit of limbo, I wasn't planning any more fertility treatment as we were thinking about our options and were taking a bit of time out. I also had to get my head around the fact that I had been diagnosed with premature menopause which would impact my fertility, what potential fertility treatment we may decide to do next and short- and long-term health implications.

Fertility Facts

POI 101

Primary Ovarian Insufficiency (POI) or premature menopause, previously known as Premature Ovarian Failure (POF) affects women under the age of 40. The term POI was first used in 1942 by Fuller Allbright, who initially reported that a small percentage of younger women experienced stopping of their periods which was subsequently caused by impaired ovarian function as a primary cause. While symptoms are often the same as in menopause, the condition is different from menopause not only because of the age of women affected but also because there is a varying and unpredictable ovarian function in around 50% of cases. (Nelson 2009)

In recent years, the known causes for POI have expanded. These causes include ovarian surgery, chemotherapy, genetic abnormalities, infection and autoimmune disorders. For around 90% of cases, the cause is unknown and remains a mystery (Nelson 2009). Therefore, unexplained POI is the most common diagnosis. The prevalence of POI in the general population is around 1% of women under the age of 40; however, new emerging data suggests that this could be much higher at around 3%. The increase is due to a variety of possible factors such as an increase in education on the symptoms of the condition and number of women having cancer treatment which then means they have POI as a result of the treatment.

While absent or irregular periods are often the first symptom, about 10% of cases patients may experience dysfunctional uterine bleeding or continue to have regular periods. Many factors influence how and where a woman might present and often a diagnosis is made just like my journey when a woman is unable to conceive. Like many other women's health conditions, many patients with POI are likely to have visited several clinicians before a diagnosis is made.

For women with the condition, there are a various treatment options to help symptoms of the condition such as mood, flushes, vaginal dryness, and irregular periods. However, it is also important that women with POI are aware of the possible long-term effects of the condition. Long-term consequences include adverse effects on cognition, bone, cardiac and sexual health. Despite significant progress in reproductive endocrinology (our hormones), our understanding of POI remains limited and the area is greatly under-researched. Change is needed in POI, research, patient care and support as well as a coordinated approach to care. At present, whilst clinical guidelines promote a woman with POI to be referred and treated under specialist care, current care is often compartmentalised or absent with many healthcare professionals only having a basic knowledge of menopause and POI.

Many women are often prescribed hormone replacement therapy (HRT) or other hormone therapy such as the contraceptive pill with limited follow-up or other supporting care offered. Conceiving a natural pregnancy if you have POI is possible but it is extremely rare, with chances of a natural pregnancy around 5%. So, as strange as it sounds, if you have POI, you still have to think about the importance of contraception if you are not planning to have a family. The best chance of having a pregnancy is with fertility treatment such as IVF using egg donation.

POI – Was It Something I Did?

It is normal to wonder when diagnosed with a life-changing condition like POI, 'Was it something I did wrong? Could I have changed something to stop it from happening?' For most of the women diagnosed with POI, the answer is no, as for a high percentage of women, the cause is unknown. Often, this can be harder on the individual level because it is human nature to look for a cause. If we find a cause, we try to solve it and look for a solution. But, this is much harder when we don't know what the cause is. What we do know from the research is that, while we don't always know a cause, some women may be born with a lower number of eggs or follicles and some women may experience an accelerated follicle depletion or dysfunction – losing more follicles along their reproductive journey than other women. Again, this is not something we usually can control. This comes down to a variety of different reasons that could include genetics, family's medical history or simply being us, being unique.

POI – How Did I Miss It?

I have thought about this over and over again, 'How did I not realise I had POI?' As a nurse who specialised in women's health working with POI patients and a variety of post-registration education, how did I not see my diagnosis? In truth, POI is not always an easy diagnosis to make. Some women don't always get the traditional symptoms we all associate with menopause hot flushes and changes in periods. Not all women who have POI will experience hot flushes or irregular periods.

For many years, before trying to conceive, I was using long-term contraception which also stopped my periods. This was also useful for my problematic periods. This meant that I wouldn't have known if my periods had changed before the coil was removed. I didn't have the typical vasomotor symptoms straight away, and cognitive changes I began to experience such as low mood, irritability and anxiety I put down to stress and the fertility journey we were on. Other symptoms such as dry itchy skin and dry eyes, I thought, were unrelated. To be honest, POI was the furthest thing from my mind.

Hindsight is a wonderful thing, and looking back, it seems obvious that symptoms were there, like pieces of a puzzle coming together. But when you are living, breathing and working in the same area, sometimes, you just can't see the wood from the trees. The fog lifted only after our second unsuccessful IVF cycle using my eggs. After that, I took a step back and started to put the pieces of the puzzle together, going back for further tests and looking at other fertility options which included egg donation.

<u>POI – How Is It Diagnosed?</u>

I can only comment on guidelines and processes in the UK as this is the country that I have predominantly practiced in over the years. We have several guidelines that can be used to aid diagnosis. This includes the NICE menopause guidelines. NICE – the National Institute of Clinical Excellence – produces guidelines for various conditions specifying the best evidence treatment. POI is covered in the NICE menopause guidelines. ESHRE – The European Society for Human Reproduction and

Embryology – also have some great POI guidelines. These are useful for both clinicians and patients and are a good place to start to find out more.

Both guidelines suggest that if POI is suspected, a hormone profile blood test should be taken around day 2–5 of your period and then repeated the following month. If you are not having regular periods, the blood test should be taken twice, 4–6 weeks apart. This hormone profile usually covers a variety of blood tests including FSH, LH, oestrogen and progesterone. These hormone tests are the basic hormones that govern your menstrual cycle. If we suspect POI, we may see an elevated FSH and a low oestrogen level. We repeat the tests because it isn't accurate to base a diagnosis on one single blood test as conditions can change. Repeating the blood tests gives us more reliability.

It is important to remember that blood tests do not give us the full picture, it is also important to look at medical history, family history and the patient as an individual asking about their symptoms and unique journey. The NICE and ESHRE guidelines give both the clinician and patient an evidence-based framework to use and a pathway for the patient.

POI – Where Might I Be Diagnosed?

You can be diagnosed with POI in a variety of clinical areas. The most common include your GP, a fertility clinic or a specialist clinic, with your GP and fertility clinic being the most common. This is because some women won't always have symptoms or may be using contraception, which masks periods or symptoms. So, women may often be diagnosed when trying to conceive as this is the time when they often stop contraception or may experience symptoms such as irregular periods or infertility.

Wherever you are diagnosed, it is important for your healthcare professional to look at the evidence-based guidelines and to consider a referral to a specialist menopause or POI clinic. Unfortunately, these clinics are few and far between within the NHS, so there may be a waiting time. A specialist clinic can offer specialist advice, treatment and long-term care for POI. Also, POI is more of an unusual condition your GP or healthcare professional may not be aware of.

Whilst there is more education and awareness, not all healthcare professionals are familiar with POI. This is why specialist clinics are important if you have POI as they have had specialist training and have experience of treating a higher number of patients with POI.

Linking back to my PhD research, education and raising awareness are crucial, especially for conditions like POI, where often healthcare professionals don't know much about the condition. Reading and reviewing current POI literature is a key part of working on my PhD. I recently read some interesting articles on POI that discussed the impact of a POI diagnosis.

Where and how the diagnosis was given had a big impact on how the patient perceived both the condition and themselves. This takes me back to my area of practice, thinking about where I had met the patients who had received their diagnosis. I even made an Instagram post once because I was so upset to hear that some women had been diagnosed with POI via text or a phone call. By raising awareness and further education, we can help practitioners understand the impact of a diagnosis, educate them and give them tools for breaking bad news and how to deliver a diagnosis in a professional and supportive way for the patients they look after.

Specialist POI Clinics

At present, there hasn't been an agreed-recorded figure of the total number of specialist POI clinics both in the NHS and the private sector in the UK. On the Daisy Network's website (the charity for POI), they have sixteen specialist POI clinics listed, with a mix of both NHS and private clinics on this list. From the patients I have seen in both a professional and support capacity, the largest and most well-known POI NHS clinics are Professor Nick Panay's Clinic at Chelsea and Westminster and Dr Lynne Robinson's Clinic at Birmingham Women's Hospital. Private clinics can vary but The Premature Menopause Clinic in Harley Street London and Hormone Health both have significant expertise and experience treating women with POI.

It is always a personal choice to decide if you will seek NHS or private treatment. This decision is multifactorial, considering factors such as waiting times, access to services, individual healthcare professionals and finances. Most patients do not have a money tree. Accessing private healthcare can be costly as it is not just the consultation appointments but also the cost of any tests and further medication or treatment that is required. My GP was not able to refer me to a specialist in POI on the NHS, and the care I received at my local NHS menopause clinic was limited at best. At that time, I was still working in a clinical nursing role and did not have much spare income. I was very fortunate that my mum has always been a great source of support and wanted to help. She paid for my private consultation with a specialist, bone density scan and initial HRT medication before my GP was able to take over prescribing my HRT.

When I see patients for a consultation, I always suggest them to try to access NHS services by asking their GP for referral. However, I know this depends on both where you live and your resources. We also know that due to the pressures of the NHS waiting times, particularly in the area of gynaecology, have also increased, which may also influence the personal decision on accessing care if you have POI.

Top Tips on Finding a POI Specialist

- Always try to see if your GP can refer you to an NHS specialist.
- Find out how long the waiting times are for both NHS and private care.
- Ask other women with POI which specialist they may have seen. The Daisy Network has a great members-Facebook page you can join once you are a member.
- Ask your chosen clinic about their knowledge and experience of treating women with POI.

For anyone starting or currently living through their fertility journey, my biggest advice would be to seek out support during the journey. When I talk about support to my patients, I often describe it as a tool kit in the back of your pocket you keep for when you need it. You may not use all the resources all at once but know that they are there when you need them and can reach into your tool kit for what you need at that time. Support can come in all shapes and sizes; it could be talking to your partner, family or friends, or it could be attending support groups, having counselling, coaching or it could be downloading an app in your phone that gives you a combination of support from forums, articles, information and experts. Many of my patients also look at other support such as meditation, reflexology, acupuncture and other relaxation techniques.

I must admit that I wasn't very proactive at seeking support. At the start of our journey, I tried to carry on as normal with the rationale that I knew about various treatments. I had seen and cared for so many patients on their unique fertility journeys. I was familiar with all the emotions, twists and turns of that roller coaster. I was open with my friends and family but didn't want to make a big deal about it. I wanted to give the impression that as both a nurse and a patient, I was in the driving seat moving forward at all times. Over time, it became harder to keep up with being 'Mrs Efficient'. Looking back, I realise I took a lot of my feelings home, often experiencing anxiety, depression, frustration and that constant pang when a friend became pregnant or had a baby.

As the weeks and months went by, I did start to seek some support, as I was undergoing treatment in the clinic. I worked with the clinic manager and the team was extremely understanding and supportive. I was offered open-ended counselling which I started to take up, finding these appointments extremely useful for my emotional mindset. In UK, all HFEA registered clinics must offer their patients access to counselling. I also made sure I had a counselling session after each failed cycle of treatment. I also started to set some protective boundaries at work. It might seem small, but I stopped going out to see patients when they brought in their babies, apart from a chosen few. This was because I would become very depressed when I had seen them with their babies. It would usually be in the evening when I got home from work once my thoughts started to process.

I think it is important to acknowledge that there is no one-size-fits-all when it comes to support and from my experience with my patients, this is something that will be different for all of us. However, as a nurse, my role was to ensure that patients knew there was support available and how to access it when they needed it. Feedback from many of my patients indicates that support is one of the most important aspects of their treatment. They want to know that support is available, how to access it and often request that more be done to explore how we can support them throughout their fertility journey. We must also remember that both patients and their partners need support and this support may not always look the same. It is important to provide support not just during the fertility journey but also afterwards, regardless of whether the journey ends with a baby. You can find out more about support options in the useful information section.

Fertility Facts
The Fertility Ladder of Treatments

There are different options when it comes to fertility treatment. I like to think about it as a step ladder: before any treatment is commenced, initial fertility pre-treatment tests are usually undertaken. For the female partner, this can include blood tests, a pelvic scan and a tubal patency test. If you have a male partner, it is important that you both are tested, and these tests can also include blood tests and a semen analysis. The results of these tests will determine the treatment options that are then offered. For some patients or couples, they can have all of the tests done and if no abnormal results are detected, they may be diagnosed with unexplained infertility. This can be a difficult diagnosis to deal with, especially when all the tests that have been done cannot find anything wrong, yet you are still unable to conceive. Other patients or couples will have a clear result from some of the tests indicating what the potential fertility problem is which will then indicate which treatment options are likely to offer the best chance of a pregnancy.

Step one on the ladder is ovulation induction. Medication can be used to provide a small amount of stimulation in a natural cycle, and the woman can have ultrasound scans also to track the growing follicle. Once the follicle reaches the required size, the patient can have timed intercourse. For this type of treatment, it is important that the male partner has a normal semen analysis and the female partner's fallopian tubes have been assessed and found to be patent (open), allowing the egg and sperm to meet.

Step two on the ladder is intrauterine insemination (IUI). This is similar to ovulation induction in the preparation with similar medication and scans at certain times of the treatment. Instead, the sperm is washed and prepared, placed in a syringe and then transferred to the uterus in a process similar to a cervical smear test. IUI can also be used if you are having treatment with donor sperm.

Step three on the ladder is Invitro Fertilisation (IVF). This is when the female partner is given stimulation medication not just to stimulate one egg but as many eggs as possible in the recruitment pool for that month or cycle of treatment. The aim is to collect multiple eggs. The eggs are collected in a minor surgical procedure known as an egg collection. The eggs are then fertilised with the male partner or donor sperm, placed in an incubator and monitored with an embryologist selecting the best embryo for transfer a few days later. If you are freezing your eggs for future, they are collected but not fertilised, and then they are frozen before fertilisation for future use.

Step four on the ladder of infertility is using donated gametes, donor eggs or sperm for your treatment. Egg donation is usually used in IVF and donor sperm can be used in both IUI and IVF. Donor eggs or gametes can also be used if you are having surrogacy treatment. It is important to understand that not everyone chooses or experiences every treatment option on the ladder, possible treatments can often depend on your circumstances and medical history.

Before starting any treatments, your fertility clinic will complete any pre-treatment tests and ask you to sign the relevant consent forms. It is rare to have a consultation and start treatment the following day. Often, treatment needs to be planned according to the start of your menstrual cycle or by using medication. You will usually be sent a treatment plan and schedule to follow once you begin treatment.

Chapter 3

Egg Donation the Last Chance Cycle

We took some time to consider our options, as no one ever wants to hear that it is unlikely they will ever have a genetic child of their own. However, we knew that we wanted to try everything we could to have a family and decided our final attempt would be IVF using egg donation. Also, from the NHS funding point of view at that time, because I had not made it to having an egg collection on our second cycle, this technically meant that the cycle hadn't been completed and I had the option of starting it again. The medical team at my clinic appealed to our local funding body, who agreed that we could have this cycle once again but as an egg donation cycle because this offered the best chances of success for Dave and I.

It took some months until an egg donor was found for us; this is a normal process, as there are often not enough egg donors available for treatment at any given time. Going back to my nursing role, I spent a lot of time running an egg donation programme and looking after recipients. I would call my recipients every few weeks with an update, even if there was a possibility there no change. I would update my recipients who were waiting with progress, where they were on the list and what the next steps were. If they were near the top of the list, I would ensure that they had all the pre-tests they needed to start treatment. Once they reached the top of the list with the help of my first work wife, we would allocate the next available donor and recipient. During the waiting time, I commenced Hormone Replacement Therapy (HRT). This helped to synchronise my menstrual cycle and also improved several symptoms which I had originally put down to stress or the fertility journey such as my mood. I continued the HRT while waiting until a potential donor was found for us or waiting for the call that might just change our future life plan.

Fertility Fact

Egg Donation

If you have POI, a natural conception is still possible. This is because the ovaries don't always completely fail, and ovarian function may be intermittent. However, the chances of a natural conception are extremely low at around 5%. This figure is also similar if you had POI and had IVF treatment using your eggs. Egg donation offers the best chance of having a family if you have POI. While, there is no guarantee, success rates are roughly around 30–40%.

Egg donation is a fertility treatment that involves a woman donating her eggs to another woman to help her conceive. The egg donor goes through part of the IVF process having medication to stimulate her ovaries to have some of her eggs collected. These eggs are then matched to a possible recipient, fertilised with their partner's or a donor's sperm and then an embryo is transferred to the recipient's uterus.

There are three types of egg donors in the UK; an altruistic egg donor, an egg sharer and a known donor.

- An altruistic donor is a woman who does not have any fertility treatment herself and wishes to donate her eggs to help others.

- An egg share donor is a woman who may already be having fertility treatment but has been allowed to keep half of her eggs for her treatment and the other half is then donated to an egg recipient.
- A known egg donor is a woman who may be known to the recipient (a sister, family member or friend) who has offered to donate eggs.

Donor eggs can either be offered on a fresh cycle of IVF or from eggs that have already been collected and frozen from a fertility clinic's egg bank. With changes in technology, it is becoming increasingly more common that the eggs are now frozen in the clinic's egg bank, these are then selected and thawed when a recipient wishes to use them.

Being an egg donor takes time.

All egg donors in the UK must be under the age of 36 and are screened following the Human Fertilisation and Embryology Authority (HFEA) requirements. This usually involves a consultation, pelvic scan, blood tests, and implications counselling. All donors in the UK must have completed relevant screening blood tests which are usually arranged by the fertility clinic. It is important to note that some of these blood tests can take a few weeks before the results are ready.

Once the initial screening has been completed, the egg donor will undergo an IVF cycle taking medication to stimulate her ovaries to produce more than one egg. The donor will then attend several monitoring scans at the clinic to assess her response and progress. After around 10–14 days, the egg donor will attend the clinic to have a minor procedure to collect the eggs. The eggs are then frozen for the clinic's egg bank or fertilised in the lab with the recipient's partner or donor sperm. The embryos are then monitored in the lab until the best day is agreed for embryo transfer. The embryo is then transferred to the recipient's uterus. Any suitable remaining embryos can then be frozen for future use by the recipient.

An egg donor is usually matched to a possible recipient using physical characteristics including height, weight, hair colour, eye colour, skin complexion, as well as the results of the screening blood tests. An IVF clinic offering egg donation usually has a specialist team who are responsible for coordinating this. From a personal point of view, I worked and helped to run an egg donation programme for many years before starting my fertility treatment. This was a rewarding role, supporting a key group of women. I was the nurse who looked after the women who were waiting for donor eggs. For some recipients, there was a significant waiting time for donor eggs to become available. So, I would get to know these patients very well, often talking to them on the phone or seeing them for regular appointments. Women need donor eggs for different reasons, not just for POI. It could also be due to age-related fertility, genetic conditions or surrogacy.

In the UK, unless it is a known donor, all egg donors are anonymous during their donation. This means that the clinic is not able to give perspective recipients any personal or identifiable information about the egg donor. They can give physical characteristics and if the donor has written a pen portrait letter (usually a short letter in the donor information form telling the recipients more about the donor), they can share this information, providing they retract any identifiable information. In the UK any child born as a result of a donation can find out non-identifiable information on their donor at the age of 16 and identifiable information when they are aged 18. Egg donors are

44

not paid; however, they can claim expenses. The IVF clinic or the HFEA can offer more information about this.

Being on both sides of the coin is a unique experience; when I would call potential recipients to offer a possible donor, it felt like one of those calls the hospital would make offering a donor a new kidney, the call they have been waiting for. You always knew that this call would usually make a recipient's day, telling them that their turn had finally come and there was a possible donor for them. Usually, they would be delighted and say, 'Tell me more!' I would then discuss the physical characteristics of the donor and answer their questions. At that point, even if they would like to accept the donor, I would still ask them to take a few days to consider the option or talk with their partner, family or friends to ensure that they were making the right decision.

As a patient, when I was on the other side of that call, honestly, I felt the same. A feeling of excitement of what was to come and a huge relief. My turn and chance to have a family had finally arrived. Even though you have never met the donor or seen a picture, you begin to build up a picture in your mind based on what the clinic tells you. I would imagine her coming in for appointments, doing her daily injections and being very aware of the path that lay ahead both for the donor and for us. Our cycle was a fresh coordinated cycle, which means that my treatment cycle was matched with the donor's cycle. We are matched together and have to get to the end of the cycle together. For the donor, this means medication to stimulate her ovaries so that eggs can be collected. For me, it meant medication to build the lining of the uterus (endometrium) to ensure that it was the right thickness to have the embryo replaced. If neither the donor nor myself were ready, the cycle would have to be stopped. Dave as the male partner, had to come into the clinic on the day of the donor's egg collection to produce his sperm sample. The sperm is then washed, prepared and analysed, ready to be used to fertilise the donor's eggs once they have been collected.

For a recipient, the cycle is much easier in terms of treatment. The medication is usually in the form of tablets or injections and there are often several pelvic ultrasounds to monitor the lining of the uterus. There is no egg collection, only the embryo is transferred at the right time. For most women, an embryo transfer is similar to a cervical smear test. Some minor discomfort but it is usually over in a short time. During the embryo transfer, you usually get to talk to the embryologists, who have been looking after your embryo and possibly see a picture. However, the emotional side can often be challenging. As a woman, I felt this was something my body was supposed to do, yet it couldn't. I then was asking another woman to go through fertility treatment and then donate her eggs, a chance to have a family, a gift where there are no words that can ever express your gratitude or appreciation.

Fertility Fact

Egg Donation and POI

At present, there are no clinically proven or effective treatments to rejuvenate ovarian activity in patients with POI. Some other treatments such as plasma replacement, which involves injecting the ovaries with plasma are the latest to be tried. Ovarian rejuvenation aims to reactivate the remaining stem cells and follicles in the ovaries to try to improve ovarian response in assisted reproductive treatments. However, this type of treatment is still experimental and there is a lack of research to determine its effectiveness and the treatment is not yet widely available. Like many other areas within women's health, more research is needed in this area.

Egg donation is currently the most successful option for fertility treatment if you have POI. Having donor eggs means that the eggs come from another woman. This woman is usually under the age of 36 in the UK and would have had all the relevant medical consultations and screening prior to donation. It is the age and quality of the eggs that are the important factor as women with POI have a very low chance of a natural conception using their own eggs.

Egg donation has a long history with the first recorded case in 1983. Doctors and scientists learnt from early egg donation cycles that if the uterus received the right preparation, then an embryo that wasn't genetically related to the donor could be implanted and develop into a healthy pregnancy and baby. The number of egg donation cycles is increasing worldwide. Today, the science of egg donation and other fertility treatments has significantly evolved.

In the UK, all fertility clinics are licensed and regulated by the Human Fertilisation and Embryology Authority (HFEA). This includes all egg donation treatments. In the UK, it is not possible to donate gametes anonymously and egg donors are not able to be paid, they can only receive a compensation payment of up to £750.00 at the time of writing. In the UK, an egg donor does not have any parental or legal rights to children born as a result of their donation. We have previously discussed what information a child born from donation can find out about their donor. In the UK, egg donors can find out the number of children born following their egg donation, their gender and the year they were born.

Initially, egg donors and egg recipients were synchronised. This means that treatment for the donor and the recipient were planned at the same time, like two branches of a tree. They both had to reach the same point and pass the same milestones for treatment to continue. The donor has to be ready for treatment and then respond to the stimulation treatment and the recipient has to be ready for treatment and ensure their endometrium (lining of the uterus) is of the right appearance and thickness. Once both are ready, egg collection can be planned and then the eggs are fertilised with the partner or donor sperm and an embryo transfer can be planned.

With improvements in freezing techniques, this means that while live synchronised cycles can still happen, clinics are now able to collect the eggs from the donor and freeze them prior to the recipient having treatment. The donor goes through her treatment and then the eggs are frozen in the clinic's egg bank and then allocated to a recipient at a later date. From a recipient point of view, this means that the recipient is aware of the number of eggs they have been allocated to before treatment and can then plan their treatment at a time that works for them.

Chapter 4

Beating the Odds

A special lady was found for us, and treatment began. We were honoured and humbled that this lady was willing to help us in our fertility journey by donating some of her eggs. Treatment began, I took the medication (tablets and vaginal pessaries) at the right time, following the treatment plan I had written many times for my patients. I went for the scans and things moved forward as planned. Dave then attended on the day of the donor's egg collection to produce his sperm sample. We went to McDonalds on the way home for a brunch then went home and waited for the call from the embryologists. When that call finally came six eggs were collected. The following day, we had another good news call; five of those eggs had formed viable embryos and we went back to the clinic. A few days later, when one embryo was transferred on day five, known as the blastocyst stage, and one embryo was frozen for subsequent treatment. When I looked at the pictures, these embryos were beautiful, textbook blastocysts that looked so different from my embryos that were transferred in our first cycle.

We then had the longest time of our lives ahead of us known as the two-week wait, the time after an embryo transfer where you have to wait to see if the treatment has worked. If you ask someone who has had fertility treatment about the two-week wait, they might tell you several things including how long those two weeks feel, how they were unsure of how to pass the time, the joys of taking progesterone medication (whether vaginally, rectally as a cream, pessary or in the form of injection), and the challenge of resisting the urge to take a pregnancy test before the scheduled date. A few weeks after the embryo was transferred, we were delighted to find that I was pregnant.

Fertility Facts

The Embryo's Journey

Whether you are having an IVF with your eggs or eggs from an egg donor, the cycle remains same. Once the eggs have been collected, your embryologist is your new best friend and possible earliest babysitter. These highly skilled scientists then put the eggs and sperm together either for IVF where the eggs and sperm are placed in a dish and allowed to fertilise on their own, or by using intracytoplasmic sperm injection known as ICSI, where each egg is injected with a chosen sperm.

The eggs are then placed in an incubator (a warm and cosy dark place) in a special fluid and then checked the following day to see how many of the eggs have fertilised. IVF is a numbers game, we don't expect all the eggs to fertilise and grow. It is normal that some won't fertilise and some won't continue to grow. Eggs which continue to grow normally are monitored in the lab until they are ready for transfer. The embryos go on a journey, the cells get developed and divided each time before they are checked again by the embryologists. For the first two days, the embryologist can count the cells developing and dividing in the embryo. From day 4, division happens quickly. By day 5, the embryo becomes a blastocyst with many dividing cells. We can visibly see certain structures including the inner cell mass which goes on to form the baby and the cells on the outside of the embryo known as the trophectoderm which goes on to form the placenta.

You can transfer an embryo usually on days 2, 3 or 5. The right date for an embryo transfer is personal to you, the number of embryos, their grading by the talented embryologists and the right day. If you are having fertility treatment, your embryologist will keep in regular contact with you discussing the best day to transfer the embryo. It is also normal that not everyone who has an IVF cycle has a surplus embryo or embryos to freeze after a cycle of treatment. This is because generally only top-quality embryos can be frozen so that they give the best chance of surviving the freeze and thaw process. Your embryologist will let you know if you have any subsequent embryos that can then be frozen. These embryos can then be thawed and used in a subsequent frozen cycle in future treatment.

Finally, test day arrived, I had resisted the urge to test early, even taking a pregnancy test was a drama. Dave ran a cross-country race in the morning with the running club. I went to watch it at a local nature reserve and I sat drinking hot chocolate and waving out of the coffee shop window as it was a cold Sunday in February. Once we got home around lunchtime, we decided to be brave and take the test. The test was a normal urine pregnancy test similar to the ones you can get from the chemist or shops. I followed the instructions, leaving the test a few minutes before I looked to see if there was a magic second line. I looked down at the two windows and only saw 1 line, it was as same as all the other pregnancy tests I had taken over the years. My initial thought was, *Oh well, at least I know now and can take my time to grieve and get my head round it.*

I called Dave to show him the test and told him that I didn't think it had worked. He asked to see the test, I showed him the test going back to sit in the bedroom. He quietly came and said, 'I think you read the test wrong.'

'No,' I said. I told him that there was only one line.

'Now there are two lines,' he said.

I couldn't believe what I was hearing. He put the light on and placed the test under the light – a faint line was visible. This was the first time I had ever seen two lines on a pregnancy test that I had taken for myself. The line was faint but it was definitely now there and I knew from my experience as a nurse that generally a line is a line!

Because the line was faint and I was scheduled to work at the clinic the following day, I spoke with one of the doctors at the clinic. They decided to give me a blood test to check my BHCG levels. BHCG is the hormone you start to produce when you are pregnant. Generally, if you take a BHCG blood test, you usually repeat it around 48 hours later as we expect the BHCG level to roughly double in 48 hours if it is an ongoing pregnancy. I had taken the test and once the results were in, it was around 56. I was pregnant! There is no agreed level and numbers don't always tell us the full story. I had the blood test repeated two days later, and my levels were now over 200 – I was still pregnant. The odds were stacked against us, but we truly believed our lives were about to change forever.

Fertility Fact
The Two-Week Wait

After you have had your embryo transfer, there is a waiting game to find out if the treatment has been successful. This time period is known as the two-week wait because it is usually around 12–14 days before you can find out the outcome of treatment. After you have an embryo transfer, the clinician will tell you what medication to continue with and what day you can take your pregnancy test. Usually, the pregnancy test is a urine pregnancy test, or on occasions, your clinician may ask you to take an HCG blood test and let you know the result. Usually, a urine pregnancy test is the most common type of test used on the test day.

The embryo needs time to talk to your uterus. There isn't any other treatment or monitoring that can tell us if treatment is successful. It is important to take your pregnancy test on the day that your clinician tells you because testing too early may not give you an accurate result. This can be for a variety of reasons; sometimes, it is too early to test so the result may not be accurate, or sometimes, if you have had an egg collection, you may have been given an HCG for your trigger injection. This trigger injection means that the eggs can be ready and collected at the right time. However, if you test early, you may still pick up traces of the trigger injection which may also make the result inaccurate. Although it is very tempting to test early, if you can hang on until your test day, this will mean that the pregnancy test is taken at the right time in your journey. If you experience any symptoms such as pain or bleeding, contact your clinician who can advise you further.

Many patients have the dilemma of what to do during the two-week wait; to be busy or to stop? And the short answer is that there is no right or wrong. Some patients take time off from work and enjoy a break away or time at home at a slower pace. Other patients continue with their normal lives and work, as they find it easier to keep busy. It is a personal decision, a case of listening to your body and how you are feeling. Another good tip is to reach into that support toolkit in your back pocket we talked about earlier. You might want to talk to the counsellor or chat with friends or family. For me, I carried on working and living a normal life. At this point, I felt very active and wanted to keep myself busy so that the time would fly by. It didn't but at least being busy helped take my mind off things and counting down until test day.

Chapter 5

Things Start to Change

Only a few days after the positive pregnancy test, I started to feel very unwell, and as the days went by, I got sicker and sicker to the point that I thought I might not recover. I experienced horrible symptoms that affected different parts of my body ranging from pelvic pain, a severe skin rash, burns on my skin, severe genital swelling, hot flushes, extreme weight loss, sickness, anxiety, low mood and panic attacks.

The symptoms seemed to happen in stages coming in like waves on a beach. I remember administering my vaginal progesterone pessary one morning and having some pain in my labia (the outside skin of the genitals). I didn't think anything of it but over the day, it began to itch, then became painful and hot. The itching increased to the point where it was all I could think about and struggled to sit down. I remember going to work a few days after, crying in the nurses office because my genitals were so itchy and painful, it felt like they were burning from the inside.

This continued for a few days, I used home treatments such as sitting on ice packs, moisturisers, regular showers and cool baths which did help but the itching and pain just seemed to get worse and then resulted in severe genital swelling and intense heat throughout my pelvic area. After a few days, I visited my GP who suspected thrush and advised me to use Canesten (the cream that treats thrush). I knew it wasn't thrush but I was prepared to try anything just to feel more comfortable. The thrush cream didn't help. By the weekend, I was getting worse. I was sitting in cold baths for hours or continually on ice packs. I visited my local NHS walk-in centre, and the nurse there was lovely. She noted that by then my blood pressure was extremely low, I wasn't able to walk that well and I had ketones in my urine – hardly a surprise as I was also not eating or drinking much at this time. She then examined me and was very surprised with what she saw; she took a swab sample and asked the on-call doctor to come in and review me. The doctor suspected a possible allergic reaction and prescribed steroid tablets which I also commenced and recommended a referral to a gynaecology specialist.

By the early part of the week, I still didn't feel any better. My nurse colleagues at the fertility clinic changed my vaginal medication to progesterone injections to see if this would help stop the local genital symptoms and asked a local gynaecology consultant to see me at the hospital. I knew this wonderful doctor very well as she worked at the clinic where I had treatment and had managed all my fertility procedures. She was kind, compassionate and one of the loveliest doctors I had the privilege of both working with and being one of her patients. She took a look at me and immediately asked another consultant colleague to review me. Both were lovely as I sat there in tears, waving a fan on a February morning in the hospital because I was so hot and uncomfortable. I was given more steroids and creams for the pelvic and vaginal symptoms, neither were sure why it was happening but hoped this would treat the problem.

At this point, although I was walking like John Wayne and had experienced a rough couple of weeks, I thought that I was now on the home straight. With the new medication, we could now focus on me getting better, moving forward and enjoying the pregnancy. I know, we shouldn't have but we took another pregnancy test. The line was no longer faint, it was bold and came up within seconds and for a day or so that's what happened. We rested and started to enjoy the time. The genital symptoms started to slowly improve and I wasn't using the ice packs as often, a glimmer of hope was peeping in.

We then went to visit my husband's family to share the good news as we hadn't told anyone about our positive pregnancy test. It was while we were visiting them that I started to feel strange. I felt hot all over like a fire was burning inside and all areas of my skin began to itch. I remember moving to sit on the floor in front of the patio doors as it was February and they were really cool. I sat in front of the patio doors for a while and eventually asked Dave if we could go home, thinking I was just tired or it was the medication I had been taking, but things only got worse. I felt hot, had a headache and my skin had turned red and began to itch and blister all over. By the morning, I hadn't slept a wink all night and I was sitting in yet another cold bath with a rash running down from my head, neck to my torso.

I continued this way for a few more days. These were the black days I still don't like to think about. All I remember is heat, pain, no sleep and an extreme fear about what was happening and what might happen. It was also unfortunate timing that Dave was working nights at this point. He had been working a 3-night shift pattern for many years, so this was the norm. Yet, it was during the night that I felt the most unwell – things always seem worse in the early hours of the morning, don't they? If I did manage to sleep a little, I would wake up in severe pain, screaming. Once the ice pack or wet towel I was sleeping on wore off, I would just run round the hall crying in pain before jumping in a cold shower multiple times during the night, not an experience I would like to repeat. One evening was so bad, it just seemed like whatever I did I just couldn't cool down. It was winter, February time, and it was cold outside, so I sat in my back garden in just a T-shirt. I was looking at the night sky, watching my breath. It was then I made peace with myself. I counted my pulse which was over 120 beats per minute while I was sitting (a normal resting pulse is between 60–100 beats per minute at rest) and looked at myself in the reflection of the window and thought, *Wow, is this how it all ends?*

You might ask why I hadn't gone to the hospital at that point, it's a good question to ask. I can honestly say that looking back now with the lack of sleep and feeling so unwell, I wasn't thinking clearly and always had this inappropriate fear that once I got to the hospital, the medics would say that nothing was wrong with me or I am a nurse and work in fertility so I should be able to handle this. I also thought they would say as I was pregnant, the management options would be limited in terms of treatment and medication would likely just be pain relievers that were safe to take during pregnancy. I also had this deep fear that I didn't disclose to anyone else that they might ask me to consider a termination. At this point, as a mother or a mother-to-be, no matter how short that time was, you always want to put the needs of your baby first. I also justified this reason in my overworked mind and thought well if I am still here the next day, then it can't be as bad as I thought and it gives the pregnancy a chance. One day is one step closer.

Fertility Fact
Taking Medication in Pregnancy

If you are planning a pregnancy and taking medication, it is important to speak to your healthcare professional about your options as not all medications are safe to take during pregnancy. This is because there may be side effects or implications for your unborn baby. Some medications aren't safe for the developing foetus. Whilst no medication can offer 100% safety, many medications have never been tested on someone pregnant, so we may not know the interaction between both the mother and the unborn baby or what the long-term implications may be. Pregnancy is a very specific physiological process where the use of medication presents a unique challenge and concern. With an estimated 83% of women using at least one medication during their pregnancy that was either prescribed or purchased over the counter (Undela et al 2020), this is a highly important area requiring further study and research.

Many women may also need to take medication during pregnancy not just due to other medical conditions but also due to symptoms or other medical concerns that occur in pregnancy. The most common medication prescribed for a previous condition taken in pregnancy is thyroxine (Undela et al 2020) which is taken for various thyroid conditions. Around 80% of women experience nausea during pregnancy (Figueroa-Grey et al 2018). Nausea symptoms can have a significant impact on the lives of some women expecting a baby. There is limited evidence for the safety of many drugs used in pregnancy and an ongoing debate about the quality and number of current studies. Women seek information in a variety of ways and Figueroa-Grey et al 2018 research provides a much-needed view of women's experience of anti-nausea medication during pregnancy. The work showed that women want and do require symptom relief to enable them to live their lives and function at home and work. The women in the study also expressed a need for more information about the risks and benefits of anti-nausea medication, something that could be applied to other medications that may need to be used during pregnancy.

If you are taking medication and become pregnant, not all medications are unsafe. For some medications, there is good safety data and it is safe to continue as normal if you are pregnant. Medication must always be selected based on the best evidence-based literature. There are always lots of options and your healthcare professional may switch you to another medication that may still treat your condition but is safe to take during pregnancy or discuss further with the multi-disciplinary team. If you are taking a variety of medications or have a complex medical history, your medical team can discuss the options with you. It always comes down to a risks vs benefits decision, something which your healthcare professional will discuss in detail with you. As more and more individuals are taking medication and have a complex history, this is something that will need to be closer looked at and be more prevalent as the years go on.

I was still here the following day and did eventually go back to my GP. He was very good once I got to the surgery and realised how ill I was, offering more steroids, blood tests and suspecting I had reacted to the fertility medication. I visited the fertility clinic again and my colleagues were just as perplexed. It was then that we decided to stop the progesterone medication as there was no other explanation of what else it could be and by then I felt I had reached the end and couldn't go on. I knew that whilst no one, not even the doctors, knew what would happen or how my body would respond, if I stopped this medication, the outcome of the pregnancy wasn't likely to be good.

Because this was a pregnancy using egg donation, my ovaries would not be making much progesterone or possibly any and this hormone is needed for the pregnancy to continue. In a natural pregnancy after ovulation, the follicle that has grown and released the egg becomes a corpus luteum. This produces the hormone progesterone that continues to support the pregnancy until the placenta takes over at around 8–10 weeks into the pregnancy. No one can predict the future and the human body always surprises us, but I knew that stopping the medication that was so needed at this stage of the pregnancy was likely to mean that our journey could end. But we had tried different progesterone medications and there were not any other viable options at this point. In a way, it felt like I was giving up, thoughts raced through my mind at warp speed. As a potential mother, the needs of the baby surely always come first? Was there anything else I could try? Could I hold out for longer and see if things changed? What would other people think? Surely, they would think I hadn't tried hard enough or could soldier on a few more days or weeks. How could I look myself in the mirror?'

However, I was so unwell by this point that if I'm honest, I also wanted to start feeling better. It was getting to the point where I could see a path where neither of us would make it through. It was one of the hardest decisions we had to make and something I didn't take lightly being well aware of the consequences and what could happen. I did feel very selfish thinking about my own needs and health. How do you prioritise your own life over that of your unborn foetus? Like many others who have had to make this difficult decision, we knew the possible consequences and what might happen. We knew that it was most likely to mean a possible end to the pregnancy, and we secretly hoped that we might beat the odds and the pregnancy would cling on and continue, but it was a decision Dave and I took. We had no choice.

Fertility Fact

Why Do We Need Progesterone?

As a part of a woman's menstrual cycle, the ovaries produce the hormone progesterone around the time of ovulation. If you conceive naturally and become pregnant, the ovaries will continue to produce progesterone as this prepares and supports, the body for pregnancy. Progesterone is then produced by the ovaries until the placenta develops and takes over supporting the pregnancy.

If you have had fertility treatment, it is important to take progesterone medication which supports the endometrium (the lining of the uterus and the embryo). Progesterone also supports a pregnancy until the placenta develops and takes over which usually is around 8–10 weeks of pregnancy. This progesterone is usually given in the form of local vaginal pessaries which are taken daily. These pessaries are usually continued until around 8 weeks of pregnancy unless a medical professional advices anything different.

Progesterone is important because your hormones may have been downregulated during fertility treatment. This means that the stimulation drugs can be controlled and given at the right time, and the eggs collected if you are having treatment using your eggs or the embryo replaced at the right time so that your hormones don't impact the treatment cycle by appearing at the wrong time. After the embryo is transferred, your cycle may be in the state of flux or confusion. We can't ask it to pick up the reigns and start producing progesterone. It may happen naturally but there is no guarantee; therefore, supplementing your treatment plan with progesterone means that the uterus and embryo get the right hormones at the right time of the cycle and continue to do so in early pregnancy until the placenta takes over this important function.

For a patient like me having egg donation, had premature ovarian insufficiency. This means that because my periods had stopped or were very irregular, I didn't technically have a regular cycle. This isn't a problem when you are having fertility treatment because the clinic can give you medication to induce a period to plan and start the treatment. I needed to take progesterone after the embryo was transferred to support the uterus and embryo because my own body did not produce any hormones regularly or at the right time in the cycle.

What was going on? At the time, I didn't know but subsequent investigations revealed I had an unusual condition called severe progesterone hypersensitivity; we will find out more about that in the next coming chapters.

Chapter 6

Game Over

Having a Miscarriage Alone at Home Unexpectedly

A few days had passed since I stopped all the progesterone injections. I didn't feel immediately better, but I also hadn't gotten any worse and was starting to adapt to the symptoms, with a good routine of cold baths, creams and steroid tablets. I also was now able to go on regular walks which helped with my mental health. Dave was at work on a day shift (he isn't always at work I promise) and I said I would go over to one of my friends' for a cup of tea. They were all rallying round and I hadn't really been out socially so thought yes, I can manage a cup of tea with them. About an hour before I left to go to my friend's, I felt a strange sensation in my pelvic area and rushed upstairs to the bathroom. It was then I realised I had started to bleed. There was no pain, just intense bleeding. I knew in my heart it was over but just wasn't ready to tell anyone or acknowledge it, so I went round to my friend's for a cup of tea and chatted about other things, their family. I felt a little better. She would never have known and that suited me fine, I just needed some time to process things before I could acknowledge it and get my head around it.

Once I got home, I waited for Dave to get back from work. I think that was the most difficult part, having to tell him what had happened. I didn't text him while he was at work. I thought it wouldn't help or change anything so I waited until he was safely home to tell him the news I knew he wouldn't want to hear. I saw the sadness in his eyes. He was wonderful telling me that everything would be OK and we had fought the good fight, but I knew then that the journey was over.

I contacted the clinic to seek advice that I was bleeding. I knew what they would say, I had given the same advice to hundreds of patients over the years as a fertility nurse. Sadly, in early pregnancy, there is little that can be done in the first few weeks. Some patients can bleed in early pregnancy and the pregnancy can still continue and is viable. As we know, the human body can do things we can't predict. It was a case of waiting it out another week until I had my pregnancy scan for the final answer. This can be the hardest part; there is nothing neither I nor the clinic can do at this point. Time is usually the final answer. You might be thinking that I should have a scan now and find out, that would be the kindest thing to do. However, time is important; if you scan a patient too early in pregnancy, everything is so small you may not see it, and then you would have to return for further scans in a few weeks which will bring the same outcome. By waiting until at least 6 weeks, this is the time when the pregnancy can be seen on the scan to confirm if it is viable.

Fertility Fact

What Happens at an Early Pregnancy Scan

So you might be thinking why wait until around six weeks in early pregnancy before we do a pregnancy viability scan. The answer is that we want to see various important physiological structures to confirm a pregnancy is viable. These structures cannot always be seen earlier than this because they are either developing or are too small to be seen.

Let's delve into it a little more. If we scan a pregnancy at around 6–7 weeks, we can expect the following:

Gestation sac – a small sac in the uterus that should contain the pregnancy.

Foetal pole – the foetus itself. You can usually see a foetal heartbeat in the size of a little bean.

Yolk sac – a small ring-like structure that supports the pregnancy in the first few weeks before the placenta is formed and takes over.

Let's think about some of those measurements. If we measure the foetal pole at around 6 weeks of pregnancy, it is small and usually measures less than 7mm. This is tiny; if you look at a ruler, you can see just how small this is. You then realise how small the structures are in early pregnancy and the challenges of measuring them.

I have had the privilege of doing many pregnancy scans. Sadly, not all of them have that happy ending that everyone hopes for. But if I were doing a normal pregnancy scan in the fertility clinic, this would usually be around 7 weeks gestation. I would be able to see the pregnancy in the uterus, I would also expect to see the gestation sac and the yolk sac and measure the foetal pole which would have been of around 7mm. I would also be able to measure the foetal heart rate which is usually above 100 beats per minute. Seeing all these structures would confirm a viable pregnancy at the time of the scan.

What If I Don't See All of Those Structures?

Unfortunately, this can mean that the pregnancy may not be viable. Sometimes, we can only see a gestation sac with no foetal pole. Other times, there may be no foetal heartbeat or no yolk sac. The most important role is talking to the patient. This is the news that no one ever wants to hear, but as a health care professional, it must be delivered sensitively, allowing the patient and their partner time to process and ask questions. Usually, a decision is never made on a single scan, the patient may be asked to rescan in a week's time to confirm the next steps or to be referred to see a doctor or other department for further advice.

Waiting for it to be my own scan was nerve-wracking. I waited through the next week and still wasn't feeling great. By now, I had been signed off from work and was taking things one day at a time. My mum had arrived, cutting her holiday in Cornwall short to look after me. There may not be anything physically that I needed, I could manage my treatment, the baths, creams and medication, but providing support, taking me out for walks and giving Dave a well-needed break so he could rest and also grieve was much-needed. My mum stayed at our house while we went for the scan. I remember one of my oldest and closest friends texting, wishing me good luck and saying, *'You never know, you just might see the feotal pole and heartbeat,'* which was so sweet. But deep down, I already knew this was unlikely after everything that had happened. We arrived at the clinic and went straight in to have the scan. My dear friend, work wife and colleague did the scan, and it confirmed what we had feared – it was not a viable pregnancy. All three of us cried together.

Fertility Fact
Why Does a Miscarriage Happen?
Having a miscarriage is devastating for those that sadly experience it, and it is only natural that one of the first questions asked is, 'Why does it happen?' The majority of miscarriages happen in the first 12 weeks of a pregnancy and some women may miscarry before they were even aware about their

67

pregnancy. The human embryo is complex. If a miscarriage happens in the first three months of a pregnancy, one of the most common causes is often chromosomal abnormalities in the baby. This can happen at the very start of pregnancy if the pregnancy gets too much or not enough chromosomes. If this happens, the baby is not able to develop properly. A miscarriage can also happen if there is a problem with the development of the placenta. There are many reasons why a miscarriage may happen and most often, the cause may not be able to be identified.

For some individuals or couples, there is a specific cause that can be identified which include thrombophilia abnormalities, immunological abnormalities, endocrinological causes, genetic conditions or structural causes. A cause may be identified if you have suffered recurrent miscarriages. Whilst it is impossible to accept a number, your GP can refer you to see a specialist if you have a history of recurrent miscarriage and most specialist miscarriage clinics will begin investigations if you have had three or more miscarriages.

Certain things can influence your risk of getting a miscarriage. This can include advanced paternal age, weight, if you smoke or drink alcohol, medications, illicit drug use and specific long-term conditions. Speak to your healthcare professional if you have any question or want any information on how to reduce your risk with lifestyle changes.

For many years, women and couples experiencing a miscarriage, have received limited support. There is much work to do in these areas, but recently things have started to change. Zoe Clark-Coates has written several amazing books offering support on pregnancy loss and has played a key role alongside Samantha Collinge in publishing the independent pregnancy loss review, which was published in 2023. The review had 73 recommendations for the UK government to improve early pregnancy and miscarriage care.

Chapter 7

The Aftermath

Coming to terms with and accepting you have a rare condition that most people haven't heard of or know anything about isn't easy and takes time! How other people respond also can sometimes be a challenge and take time to get used to. One of the first responses that stuck in my mind was when I went for an acupuncture session. It had been a few weeks since the worst of the symptoms and I was still struggling with feeling hot, anxiety and lack of sleep. Many of my patients had used acupuncture and said they found it helpful, always telling me how much more relaxed they felt after a session and how it made a difference to them. I thought to give it a try. I booked a session with a local acupuncturist; she was a lovely, kind and an excellent practitioner. The first thing I had to ask for was about the heated blanket be turned off on the couch. At that point, I just couldn't bear any heat, it was still quite chilly outside. Early spring, yet I was walking around in light summer clothing and the thought of a heated blanket sent my flushes into overdrive. I already felt like I was in Spain and didn't want any more heat added to the mix.

During the appointment, I was asked to fill out some medical paperwork, including the usual suspects, medical history, medication any allergies and why I was there. Then the practitioner asked me to talk about it, it was quite a matter of fact. It had been a few weeks and at that point, I had cried so much in the difficult weeks before I didn't feel I had any tears left and I just couldn't show any more emotion at this point. I was brief and concise telling my story, explaining that I had fertility treatment recently and developed a rare condition which meant I lost my baby, any future fertility treatment and nearly my life over the recent weeks. I was now trying to adjust to a new norm and living with a variety of symptoms and grief. At this point, the lovely practitioner started to cry. For a minute, I thought I was in another world. 'What was going on?'

I then went into a role reversal, reassuring her, thanking her for her concern. I told her that I was fine. She must have thought that I had a heart of stone. I did manage to finish the session, feeling a little more relaxed and didn't overheat thanks to the electric blanket being turned off. I then went home with ear clamps that the practitioner said would help with my symptoms. Sadly, they just made my ears feel even hotter than before, so I removed them before bed. I didn't go back for a subsequent session; I would have found it too difficult for both us, me and the poor practitioner.

Although kind, touching and very human, you just don't expect these sorts of reactions, particularly when you are the patient. Over time, I got used to a variety of reactions which ranged from gasps, shock, that look of surprise or leading on to further questions such as "I haven't heard of that before", "How do you recover from that?", or "How do you get through each day after that?" At the time, I hated these reactions. 'Why couldn't people just pretend they knew about it or say nothing?' Now as a great deal of time has passed, I just smile or sometimes shake my head. Now that some time has passed, there just isn't the same emotional attachment or intense emotion when I talk about my journey.

Changes in Health

The first few months after the miscarriage were extremely tough on my health both physically and emotionally. I struggled with a variety of symptoms; the physical symptoms were reducing, the genital swelling was gone and the skin changes were gradually getting back to normal, although I was left with some light scarring on my neck and chest, this area even now remains red and looks a little like a light sunburn. Also, for the first time in my life, I had lost a significant amount of weight without trying. For weeks, I had no appetite and had lived on porridge and an apple most of the days, this had taken its toll and I was the lightest I had ever been, clothes just hung off me. However, the combination of both physical and emotional symptoms was extremely debilitating, I was plagued with palpitations, hot flushes, severe insomnia, panic attacks, severe anxiety and depression.

I couldn't go downstairs in the house at night because I would have flashbacks of the bad days when I had sat in the garden or the lounge for nights on end alone and in pain. When I was upstairs, I would just pace around the room. I initially tried some oral cyclical HRT I had taken prior to the treatment to help with cycle regulation and menopause symptoms, but this didn't agree with me at all this time. Around l, I experienced a severe emotional change in my mood, increased anxiety and almost a mania whilst I was taking the progesterone part of the HRT. I thought that the HRT would get me back on the track to normal again; instead, I felt more anxious than ever, couldn't sleep and felt like I was in some sort of mania. Everything was on fast forward, and I couldn't sit still and felt like my mood and emotions were running away with me. This wasn't something I could continue.

That was when I got to the very first paragraph in the book, the point of no return. By then, I had months without sleep, was experiencing severe cognitive symptoms and I just couldn't go any further. The night before, I hadn't slept at all and had considered going out and ending my life. It had to stop. What I didn't realise was that some of the emotional symptoms were likely both because of my POI and the progesterone hypersensitivity. When the GP gave me the antidepressants, this was a life changer. Whilst there is no clinical evidence to support my response, it seemed like a switch in my brain just flicked back on.

Most people take antidepressants to help with anxiety or low mood and it takes weeks or months to take effect. When I started taking the antidepressants, I started to see a change relatively quickly within about an hour. It felt like something had changed in my brain. I remember lying in our bedroom and saying to Dave, 'I feel different, it is a strange feeling, but I genuinely feel a little different than just a few hours ago.' The decision to take antidepressants wasn't an easy one to make as all medications carry risks as well as benefits, but I had to try something, or I might not have made it through that day. Things didn't completely resolve straight away but over a few months, I started to notice improvements in symptoms such as my mood and sleep. I remain on a low dose of antidepressants which for me works to keep my brain feeling more balanced and like me.

Due to progesterone hypersensitivity being so unusual, treatment and care options have to be individualised. Whilst this approach may not work for other women with the condition, for me it was a game-changer and a lifesaver. That small percentage of feeling a little more normal was enough to shift the perspective from 'How will it end?' to 'How can I begin again?'

Fertility Fact

Why Do Women with POI Take HRT?

For women with POI or premature menopause, the ovaries no longer produce the hormones needed to maintain their health and menstrual cycle. Key treatment is hormonal medication such as the oral contraceptive pill or hormone replacement therapy (HRT) which aims to top up or replace the hormones that ovaries are no longer producing. Replacing these key hormones can help with treatment of menopause symptoms, helping with both short-term and long-term symptoms.

We hear a lot in the media about menopause and HRT; however, it is important to note that younger women taking HRT present different risks and benefits. It is important if you have a diagnosis of POI that you consider taking hormone therapy until at least the age of natural menopause (around 50–52) as replacing the hormones your body should be producing can help with symptom relief and has long-term benefits.

However, it is also important to find the right medication that works for you as there is no one-size-fits-all. There are many types of HRT medication that come in different dosages and routes and sometimes you may have to try several types of medication before you find the one that works for you. Your doctor or healthcare professional can offer advice on treatment and management.

I first began counselling; I was lucky as my employer offered six sessions as part of their benefits programme at the time. I chose cognitive behaviour therapy, a type of therapy that helps you cope with your symptoms by changing the way you think and respond to them. The method in my madness was as I didn't know the path of this condition or how long the symptoms would persist, I needed to start being proactive about managing them. I saw a counsellor for six weeks and every Wednesday morning we would talk about my experiences, ways to respond to the emotions and physical symptoms. Some of these tools I still use today.

All medication, changes and interventions take time to work, and this was no different in my case. I moved forward with the medication, counselling and lifestyle changes, and over the next few months, I started to gradually see some improvements. The antidepressants immediately returned some of my sleep, reduced anxiety and helped with mood changes. Meditation and CBT techniques were also really helpful with managing anxiety. I also began using moisturisers to help with the changes in my skin. My appetite also returned full speed ahead and I began to put on the weight I had lost plus a little bit more. It is important to be honest and acknowledge that while I improved slowly over time, there were still some days that I didn't feel well or struggled with symptoms; however, over time these days became less, and I also got better at managing the symptoms.

Chapter 8

Putting the Puzzle Together

A few weeks had passed since my miscarriage, and I was still in complete denial. Firstly, I returned to work 3 days after our scan to get on with things and pretend it hadn't happened. I just wanted life to get back to normal – something familiar. I didn't want to face any more of the unknown. It wasn't easy to pretend that I was the same person; I still had a variety of symptoms. The first strangest symptom was my skin peeling off like a spider from around my neck, ears and chest, followed by severe insomnia. I would often be awake until four a.m. without any sleep, just grabbing a few hours before the alarm would go off. I would then arrive at work feeling and looking like I was in a battle zone. Suffering from the effects of the symptoms, lack of sleep and juggling an advanced nursing role was not a good combination.

After one particular day, I was sat in the scan room trying to remember where I had put some documentation. It all became a bit much and I became upset, my great friend and colleague said the words I didn't expect to hear, 'Have you thought about finding out a bit more about what happened to you?' I looked up and didn't say anything. She continued, 'No one seemed to know what the symptoms were or what was wrong with you. Don't you want to know what happened and why?'

I said I would think about it and went home. Later that evening, I did think a little more and began to do some research.

Thinking back, my good friend was right; most doctors and specialists who tried to help had the same response, 'We have never seen this before; we are not sure what is going on.' They tried to treat the symptoms, genital swelling, skin rash and burns with steroids and creams. They had also changed my progesterone from vaginal pessaries to injections to see if this made any difference. Unfortunately, it only made things worse, leading to a severe skin rash and burns. I then had more steroids, antihistamines and pain relief before I made the decision to stop the progesterone because the symptoms were too much to cope with. Being in the stages of early pregnancy I was unable to take a number of medications that might have been offered because they were not safe to take in pregnancy.

I then started to think, what could I do next? Luckily, the clinic where I worked had some private health care and I was able to access and use this to see a specialist privately whom I will refer to as "the prof". I did some research on the best and experienced expert in this area and booked a private appointment with a reproductive endocrinologist (a hormone doctor) in London the following week. Because Dave was working – again! – my mum kindly went with me. I think this was also the right thing so that Dave did not have to live out the whole journey and symptoms again. I remember meeting my mum at the tube station in London. She was wearing a lovely smart blue jacket whilst I was in a dress and trainers. Clearly, I should have thought more about my outfit!

We headed to the clinic. I did not know what to expect. Initially, it was the usual admission, paperwork, height, weight and blood pressure. We were then taken through to see "the prof", a kind and gentle man who listened to my story, asking questions along the way. I don't remember much, and at that point, I hadn't seen many specialists privately, let alone a professor. I didn't realise I was that interesting. But the moment he got his iPad out and started making notes, I felt that this was all about to change. The prof listened and the first thing he asked was if I had considered using a surrogate, as this would be the least risk for any future treatment (at this point, we still had our other remaining embryo in storage). I replied, 'No, it was not something that I thought would be right for us.'

The prof went through my medical history thoroughly, picking up some very relevant points from my history that when put all together, seemed very relevant. I had never conceived a natural or other pregnancy from any fertility treatment before, my periods even before treatment when I did have them were always extremely irregular or I often bled for prolonged periods, usually weeks rather than days. I had also had the Mirena coil for many years due to problematic periods which had been a godsend, I had often joked I would love to give a knighthood to the person or team that invented it, it really was a life saviour; having a coil meant I could live a life. I went into nursing and didn't worry about prolonged heavy periods or sitting on a white sofa. He wondered what if any little exposure I had had in my progesterone hormones.

Fertility Fact

What Is a Mirena Coil?

A Mirena coil is an intra-uterine device that can be used as a contraception, for heavy or unpredictable periods, or as the progesterone part of HRT. It is a small device that is placed inside the uterus by a specially trained doctor or nurse. The coil delivers a small dose of progesterone into the uterus that keeps the endometrium (lining of the uterus) thin. As a result, this can also mean that periods become lighter or even stop altogether. Depending on why you may have the coil fitted, it can remain in situ for several years. Your doctor or healthcare professional will advise you on how long it can remain in situ as guidelines can change.

Like all types of treatment, some women respond well to the Mirena coil, while others don't. It is important to find what works best for you. A Mirena coil can be used for various purposes, including contraception, the progesterone part of HRT and for managing heavy or painful periods. It is a highly useful option for women offering both contraception and control of their periods.

The prof also asked about the symptoms, not just the physical symptoms such as the rashes, burns and swelling but also the cognitive symptoms. He mentioned that hormones were a big part of the brain. I looked at my mum and said, "I was fine, right?" My mum began to laugh – humour is a big thing in our family. 'No,' she said, 'you were a little crazy at that point!' It is only now when I look back and realise how bad some of the cognitive symptoms were. Extreme anxiety, I would panic if Dave left the room to the point of hysterical crying, breakdown. There was a continuous low mood, suicidal thoughts, jumbled thoughts and severe insomnia which felt like a switch was missing from my brain when it came to falling asleep, it just wasn't there any more. I am sure some of that was down to stress, lack of sleep and feeling unwell but now when I look back, many of them were probably also due to the progesterone hypersensitivity, all going on not just physically but cognitively.

The prof also mentioned that if we were still considering any future treatment, a specialised treatment plan for medication would be needed, and he would be happy to help write it. He talked about doing a few practice cycles with progesterone, using steroids and anti-histamines if required for any symptoms as well as assessing my response before planning the next cycle. The ultimate aim would be to use a progesterone that I could tolerate alongside supporting medication such as steroids and antihistamines which would dampen down any reaction until the pregnancy was far enough developed that the placenta could then take over and I could then stop any progesterone medication.

I came away from the consultation experiencing mixed emotions. Firstly, I was relieved, someone understood what was happening and had seen it before. Secondly, there was hope; it would be very risky, but we could think about the option of trying treatment again. I might not have to give up on that last beautiful embryo that was currently in storage. Thirdly, I had some of his words in the back of my mind – using a surrogate would be the option offering the lowest risk and recovery from the current symptoms I was experiencing. It might take time but there was no set path.

The prof also wrote to my GP with a consultation summary. This was very helpful. Whilst my GP had been supportive from the blood tests to the treatment, he then found it hard after the miscarriage when I was still going back with symptoms such as insomnia, skin changes, depression and anxiety. Having the letter provided guidance and further important information, something that wasn't in his specialty. He must have been surprised as he rang me at home when I hadn't planned an appointment to discuss the letter further and reassure me that he would support any recommended management. It was good to finally have some answers.

After finally receiving a diagnosis, I began to see the

positive. A diagnosis gives your symptoms meaning, and I realised it wasn't just in my head. Although I wasn't miraculously healed and still experienced symptoms, I felt better knowing I had information, resources and a plan to move forward. It wasn't too much to ask but it was vital for the future. I then began to read and research further about the role antidepressants can play for some women with premenstrual dysphoric disorder (PMDD) – a severe form of PMS – and then something clicked in my head. Patients with PMDD would often take the antidepressant to regulate the neurotransmitter dysregulation and they would often feel better within hours, unlike patients who take antidepressants for depression or anxiety which can often take a few weeks to see any benefits. This was what had happened to me within a few hours. I felt like something had changed, I even emailed the prof to tell him how I couldn't believe how much better I felt and how I had slept for the first time in months. I don't think he was surprised as I remember his email reply telling me not to worry about the anti-depressants as they were likely helping with the progesterone sensitivity.

Fertility Fact

Why We Don't Always Have the Answers?

We now live in a world with many great advances in modern medicine, and so much good has been done with recent medical advances and discoveries. It might be safe to think that we have all the answers but in reality, there is so much that we don't know about the human body, and the area of fertility is no different. Fertility is relatively a new area of medicine that only began to significantly advance in the 1960s and 1970s.

The first test tube baby 'Louise Brown' was born in 1978. So when we think about IVF, it has only been around for a very short time, even though this was before I was born – just over forty years. 'Isn't that long?' Whilst technology is changing and advancing, there is still so much that we don't know. We talked about unexplained fertility earlier in a fertility fact. The fertility industry is highly regulated and there are strict rules on the storage and use of embryos. Whilst great work has been done and is still being done, there is still so much that we don't know when it comes to fertility. Hopefully, over time, we will find out more answers so that we can help our future fertility patients.

This was one of the reasons we decided to donate our embryo to research, as it allows researchers the opportunity to use these embryos for their research projects. Without this opportunity, they would not be able to get closer to the answers. Choosing to donate your gametes is a personal choice and not something that is right for everyone. I would always suggest you to take time to consider this decision, speak to your clinician, and make sure you have relevant information and counselling to help you feel informed. However, it may just be a gift that could help future fertility patients.

Chapter 9

Progesterone – What We Know

Now I switch to Kate, the reluctant academic, and we take a look at the history of progesterone, what we know and how things have changed over the years.

The history of progesterone is old but remains in progress (De Renzo et al, 2020). Progesterone is the oldest female hormone that we first learnt about. The term progesterone literally means for pregnancy and should only be used to refer to the natural hormone produced by the ovaries or included as part of a drug. The modern history of progesterone began way back in the 1600s when physician and anatomist Regnier de Graaf observed the presence of a corpus lutea in the cows' ovaries which correlated with a pregnancy. The term 'hormone' was first used by British physiologist E H Sterling in 1905 which explained the chemical messenger action produced in glands that are transported via the bloodstream. The hormone was officially documented in medical journals from 1929 onwards.

Willard Allen – an American gynaecologist – and George Corner – a professor of anatomy – detailed the first and second manuscripts describing the role of the corpus luteum in rabbits and their role in the implantation of the embryo. In a subsequent paper "My life with Progesterone", Allen reflected on the day when he isolated progesterone. Initially known as corpus luteum hormone, in 1935, a decision on the name progesterone was then given for the hormone. Research on this new hormone continued, and at first, it was very difficult to synthesise and produce and that's why the costs remained high. In the late 1930s, progesterone could be extracted from a species of wild yam in Mexico, known as the Dioscorea. This could be converted into the hormone using a cheaper technique making progesterone widely available for researchers and pharmacists. By the early 1950s, progesterone became more mainstream with the first oral contraceptive being developed from progesterone.

Progesterone is a hormone that is mainly secreted from the corpus luteum (the follicle that contained the egg prior to ovulation) in the ovary during the second half of the menstrual cycle (known as the luteal phase). It plays an important role in the menstrual cycle, preparing the body for a possible pregnancy, supporting and maintaining a pregnancy in the early stages. During the second phase of the menstrual cycle, the impact of progesterone leads to changes in the thickening of the endometrium (lining of the uterus) so that possible embryo implantation can take place. In addition to reproductive functions, it is also thought that progesterone has anti-inflammatory properties and plays a role in our immune system.

In addition to the ovaries and the placenta, some progesterone can also be produced in the adrenal glands and the brain. Progesterone is synthesised by two enzyme steps. Step 1 is the conversion of cholesterol to pregnenolone in the mitochondria. Step 2 is the conversion from pregnenolone to progesterone by another enzyme 3B hydroxysteroid dehydrogenase. The synthesis of progesterone is relatively simple in the human body compared to other hormones such as oestrogen; however, there is no one-size-fits-all when it comes to hormone levels that are produced.

The research leading to the discovery of progesterone and some of its key functions was fuelled by the curiosity and skill of physiologists, pathologists and embryologists wanting to learn more about this unique hormone and explore the link between the uterus and pregnancy. Progesterone is only present in the luteal phase of the menstrual cycle and during pregnancy. Progesterone also plays a key role in the maintenance of the uterus during pregnancy. It prevents muscle contraction and stimulates blood vessels that supply the endometrium. Once pregnancy is established, progesterone is essential for immunotolerance and also helps to maintain the cervix. It is also thought that progesterone also functions as a vasodilator which can also help to reduce blood pressure.

Progesterone also provides other positive effects on a woman's health including some cardiac protection, the neuroprotective effects of progesterone have also been demonstrated, and we also know that progesterone prevents sleep disturbance. I have seen this in practice many times over the years when caring for ladies on their menopause journey, for some ladies taking oral micronized progesterone a newer type of natural progesterone derived from plants, in particular the yam, it is identical to the structure of the hormone progesterone because of this it is often referred to as body identical. Utrogestan can radically improve some women's sleep, which is why it is recommended it be taken at night.

As progesterone is a steroid hormone, it can easily pass through the blood-brain barrier. In women, the regions of the brain with the highest concentration of progesterone are the amygdala followed by the hypothalamus. It is also thought that progesterone influences other behavioural circuits in the brain such as the GABA-R receptors. Binding to these receptors may have a sedative and neuroprotective effect. Things are even more complex with recent studies demonstrating that progesterone can act as modulators for other neurotransmitter systems in the brain. However, this is a complex area requiring further research. Like oestrogen, we also have progesterone receptors throughout the body.

In recent years, the use and role of progesterone has increased from contraceptives to fertility treatment, IVF treatment, recurrent miscarriages and pre-term births. Over time, significant advances have been made in the formulations of progesterone medication and administration options for patients. These clever scientists, doctors and professors worked on finding out about this important hormone, how to produce and synthesise it to use it in a variety of medications and treatments. Progesterone is important for both women's health and reproductive health. As always, further research will contribute to a better understanding of the role of progesterone which will tell us more about the hormone, its impact and its use on treatment for women. Previous and clinical developments with progesterone are indeed a never-ending story (Piette, 2018). As we are finding out that all of us are unique as individuals and how women react to different hormones can vary, there truly is no one-size fits-all.

Fertility Fact

Progesterone Fun Facts
- First discovered in 1929.
- Scientifically known as P4 on blood tests.
- After ovulation, when progesterone is produced, there is a 0.3–0.5 degree increase in body temperature.
- Progesterone can bind to GABA receptors in the brain.
- Progesterone literally means for pregnancy.
- It is thought that progesterone may play a role in bone density; however, more research is needed in this area.

Chapter 10

Progesterone Hypersensitivity

From what I have learnt from my reading and consultations with experts, progesterone hypersensitivity is a relatively new and rare condition that occurs due to a reaction to endogenous (a patient's hormone) or exogenous progesterone (progesterone from medication or outside the body). First identified in 1964 by Shelley et al, it was previously known as autoimmune progesterone dermatitis. The condition was renamed progesterone hypersensitivity (PH) because it reflected the heterogeneity of its presentation. Endogenous PH is usually a collection of symptoms that is present during the luteal phase of a woman's menstrual cycle. Exogenous PH symptoms occur following the use of a progestin medication such as hormonal contraception, hormone replacement therapy (HRT) or fertility medication.

Progesterone is a steroid hormone derived from cholesterol. It has multiple metabolic and physiologic effects related to the menstrual cycle. Classic PH typically presents as cyclic dermatitis (skin rashes) that occurs in the luteal phase (after ovulation) of the cycle due to an increased level of progesterone. However, with the increased use of exogenous progestins ranging from contraceptive medication, and fertility treatments such as in-vitro fertilisation (IVF) which uses high dosages of progesterone to support a potential pregnancy, there is likely to be an increase in the prevalence of PH in the future. It is important to note that progesterone medications are used by millions of women around the world for a variety of reasons ranging from fertility treatment, part of HRT treatment or contraception, and currently, there are fewer than 200 cases of PH described in medical literature (Foer and Buchheit 2019). Risk factors for developing PH include fertile age, prior use of exogenous progestin and pregnancy. PH is not reported to be a familial disorder, although further research is needed in this area. Data suggests that PH typically occurs in women who are of childbearing age with most women presenting in their 30s.

Sex hormones are closely related to the development and regulation of our immune system which has sex hormone receptors and responds to hormonal signals. The pathogenesis of PH in humans remains unclear. It is often observed that women diagnosed with the condition may experience it later in life, typically in their 30s. This suggests that they might initially tolerate low levels of the hormone but develop an inflammatory response as hormone levels rise during certain physiological stages. As progesterone rises both in the luteal phase of the cycle and in pregnancy, the levels are then much higher and individual to each patient.

Because symptoms can vary, it can be a challenging diagnosis to make. Key symptoms can vary in severity and presentation but can include periodic skin rashes, hives, urticaria, erythema breathlessness, cough and anaphylaxis, with the most common reported symptoms being urticaria and erythema because the skin often shows signs of hypersensitivity more than any other organ in the body. It is important to be aware that not all patients presenting with PH will experience skin rashes, and some can develop a delayed response often several days later.

PH can also develop without previous exposure to progestins. Possible theories for PH include an immunoglobulin E (IgE) medicated response which is the most widely accepted theory. Another possible theory is antibodies that are formed in response to medication, food or infection. These have been proposed as a possible cause because they may cross-react with progesterone.

Diagnosis is based on clinical history, physical examination and in some cases the use of an intradermal progesterone skin test; however, it is important to note that not all patients with PH will have a positive skin test. Foer et al (2016) suggested that only 50% of patients have a positive result. In response to the limitations of a skin test, Gosh and Bernstein (2019) recently developed a progesterone-specific IgE assay in the form of a bovine serum albumin known as ELISA, that could be used for diagnosing patients with suspected PH. Their study results for patients who were tested using the assay ranged from high positive to low positive and negative offering an alternative positive predictive value for screening women with potential PH. It is also important to exclude other disorders that may mimic PH symptoms.

Possible treatment focuses on controlling the symptoms or inducing anovulation. Treatment options can range from steroids, antihistamines or progesterone desensitisation therapy. Desensitisation therapy offers women with PH the option to tolerate fertility treatments and pregnancy, especially for those seeking to conceive. It can also be considered for symptom control. Desensitisation protocols can be given orally, vaginally or through intramuscular injections depending on patient or clinician choice. There are other options for treating PH that would have significant effects on fertility; these include using downregulation medication which can stop a woman's cycle or the surgical option of an oophorectomy (removal of the ovaries) which is often seen as a last resort.

Management is usually led by the patient's goals and choice. If the patient's goal is symptom control, therapies such as antihistamines or suppression of ovulation may be a good option. For patients seeking pregnancy or when conventional treatments do not provide symptom relief, desensitisation therapy is likely to offer the safest and most effective treatment for the condition.

Because the condition is rare and so little is known about it, there are no specific support groups charities or information to sign-post patients. It is likely that women suffering from the condition may not know of any other patients with a similar diagnosis. Women must be offered appropriate support such as counselling or referred to the appropriate speciality for individualised care. Further, long-term research and clinical trials are recommended.

Due to the increased use of exogenous progesterone in fertility treatment such as IVF, HRT or contraceptive treatment, there is likely to be an increase in cases in the future. Education and raising awareness of the condition with health care professionals is vital to prevent delay in diagnosis, treatment and to offer support to women with the condition. At present, PH has not been seen in menopausal women who are receiving progestins as part of their HRT treatment. A collaborative care approach is recommended in complex cases with various medical specialists including gynaecologists, reproductive endocrinologists, fertility specialists, immunologists and primary care doctors.

Despite being around since the 1960s, the prevalence of PH remains unknown. Some skin and blood tests have been developed to aid a diagnosis alongside a clinical history and symptoms experienced. Medical management and desensitisation are the most successful and regularly used treatment for PH. Recent studies demonstrated a new anti-IgE medication known as omalizumab that has shown a successful treatment of PH; however, further research using this medication is needed.

The variety in how patients present with PH and the varied responses to treatment make it a challenging condition to manage. However, looking at some of the research, there appears to be some common factors with the condition:

1. The condition usually affects women of reproductive age with typical age being in their 30s.

2. The condition may appear around 10 days before a woman's period (in the luteal phase of the cycle).

3. When associated with pregnancy, it may continue after the baby is born.

4. In around half of the patients diagnosed with the condition, exposure to external progesterone (medication) had occurred.

5. The majority of patients experienced some skin complaints such as skin rashes or itching.

6. Analysis of the research suggests that the condition is multi-factorial.

Clinical Trial for One?

Because it is a rare condition and there are not large amounts of women presenting with this condition, this does subsequently limit what clinical trials can be done. However, looking at the research does give me hope that we might eventually find out more about this unusual condition. I read in a recent review that a model had been developed to study oestrogen hypersensitivity. The reviews theorised that this model could be used to study the effects of PH. The most recent article I read (Patel et al 2023) suggests that although there has been an increased awareness in the medical literature, an improved understanding of the pathophysiology and more commercially available tests are needed, along with a specialist's referral for patients with the condition. Future research and studies have the potential to advance our understanding of this rare condition, which could, in turn, improve its management and help with possible treatment options.

Chapter 11

Donating Our Embryo

We juggled many different emotions in the months during and after my recovery. After consulting our reproductive endocrinologist whom I refer to as the "Prof", we had to make the difficult decision of whether further treatment would be possible. We still had one beautiful embryo frozen and in storage. Of course, it was a beautiful high-grade blastocyst, it hadn't come from me. I would look at the picture over and over again, wondering if we could give it a try. But I knew deep in my heart it wasn't an option. One thought that kept echoing in my mind was the first thing the prof said after explaining what he believed had happened to me and diagnosing the condition: 'Why don't you use a surrogate?' That would be the less risky approach.

In medicine and healthcare, we always think about risks vs benefits. What are the risks of the treatment or condition and what are the benefits? Using a surrogate to carry our embryo would not mean any further risk for me. I knew that it was just something I couldn't do and something that wasn't right for me. In my head, it just didn't add up. I had got my head around using donor eggs, although any child wouldn't be genetically related to me, I would carry the baby and I would experience the pregnancy. If we used a surrogate, I would be like an unwanted guest at a party. While surrogacy is a viable option and works for many people, it just wasn't something that would work for me. Dave didn't want me to go through fertility treatment again; after all, look what had happened the last time. So, we were at loggerheads, I didn't want to use a surrogate and he didn't want me to have any further fertility treatment. We gave it more time; after all, the embryo was stored safely in the freezer and time was something that we did have. We finally both agreed we would take that difficult step and decided that would be the end of our fertility journey. In January 2018, we made the decision to donate our embryo to research.

I was determined to end on a positive note after the ordeal we had been through, so I initially inquired about donating our embryo to another couple, giving them the gift of a family and a chance at parenthood. However, this was not possible for us because we had only one embryo. Generally, fertility clinics suggests couples or any person to donate multiple embryos as this gives a potential recipient a better chance of success. Anxious not to discard our embryo, we decided that we would donate our embryo for research, knowing it would be helping future generations. I can't thank our special embryo mums enough – the lovely embryologists who looked after us and our embryos during all of our cycles, you know who you are, and thank you for going above and beyond to ensure our embryo got sent for research as it wasn't something the clinic did regularly at that time. At around this time, we had also decided that adoption or fostering wasn't right for us. This meant we had closure. Although it was difficult but a relief now that we had decided as we didn't feel we were in limbo any more and could finally start moving forward.

Fertility Fact
Donating an Embryo – What Does it Mean and What Is the

Process?

Embryo donation is possible when surplus frozen embryos remain after an IVF cycle. Usually, embryos are donated after a couple has completed their cycle of treatment. Patients or couples can decide if they wish to keep their remaining frozen embryos in storage for future treatment or if they wish to donate their embryos to give other individuals or couples a chance to have a family. There is also the option to donate embryos for research projects.

If you have frozen embryos in storage and would like to donate them to others to give them the opportunity to start a family, you will normally have to have two or more embryos in storage. This would allow the patient whom you are donating to have the best chances of success. Ideally, the age of the egg donor needs to be between 18–35 years at the time the embryo was created. The patient or couple choosing to donate the embryos will then attend the clinic for an assessment of their health and medical history and an implications counselling session to discuss the implications of donating the embryos. They would also have specialist blood testing to reduce the risk of passing on any other medical conditions to any children born as a result of their donation.

Like all other donations in the UK, the donation will be anonymous at the time of treatment; however, any child born as a result of your donation can receive identifying information on their donor when they reach the age of 18. If you donate your embryos, you will have no legal parental responsibilities for any children born as a result of your donation. You are also able to find out if your donation was successful. Donating embryos is a personal choice and you must take time to consider this important decision and undertake the relevant tests, medical screening and counselling which is part of the process. However, it can offer other individuals and couples the option to have a family. Embryo donation can help a variety of individuals or couples, this can include couples who may have had multiple unsuccessful IVF cycles, single women, same-sex couples who may be using a surrogate or if a couple has a serious medical condition that could be inherited.

Chapter 12

A Husband's Perspective
Dave – How Did He Cope?

So, what would I say about the love of my life? Well, he is just about the opposite of me in every way. I am short, busty and can be a bit of a whirlwind. Dave is tall, bald, handsome with the most amazing eyes and calm demeanour. He has a love of video games and Marvel films and has a gift for problem-solving and using technology. He is extremely bright, much cleverer than me but is also dyslexic so doesn't enjoy reading or writing. He works as a technician in manufacturing which whilst may not be his job of choice probably plays to some of his strengths – problem solving, teamwork and technology. Like all of us, he isn't perfect, he can be stubborn, has a wicked sense of humour and can sometimes sulk if life isn't going his way.

We had both been married before, and when we met, we began a long-distance relationship. I was living and working in the Midlands and Dave was living in Harwich which was a three-hour drive away. After a year of visiting each other and spending a lot of time on the A14, we decided to move in together and I made the move to Harwich as it was easier as a nurse to find a job in another location. A second time around wedding was the best; being older and wiser, I wasn't afraid to think outside the box and have a wedding that we wanted and worked for us rather than conforming to expectations. We got married at our local boutique cinema. I wore a green sequined dress and we had a vintage shabby chic theme wedding, watching the film *Love Actually* after the ceremony, followed by afternoon tea at a local hotel with our close family and friends. It was a day to remember that didn't break the bank but was completely us.

It would be easy to focus on my own experience. However, I would be missing one of the most important people of the journey, my beloved husband Dave. Often, men can be overlooked when we talk about fertility and pregnancy loss, but their experiences are just as important. Dave had gone through the journey and was there with me every step of the way, yet he had his own battles during the journey. He had a wife with a variety of health issues that he had to help nurse back to health, and no baby – not the outcome he would have wanted. He had a wife who would tell him to leave and find someone else with whom he could have children. Dave isn't much of a talker, particularly about our experience, so it took me a while to get him talking and when he did, it wasn't much with a lot of me asking him questions to draw the information out.

I think that everyone is different and men generally respond differently to that of women. I might be generalising, but men often don't always talk to their friends or seek out counselling and Dave also followed this pattern. But over time, he found his way through. Getting our dogs really helped him, as it got him outside more, exercising and walking them. This, in turn, led him to meet more people. You talk to people when you have a dog as you meet them on your walk. Although he went to a couple of fertility counselling sessions with me and he doesn't talk about our journey that much, but when he does, he always says that he was glad because we were both still here and have each other.

Dave found the fertility journey an interesting one. He

always jokes that he didn't do much on the fertility journey as most of the tests are focused on the female partner. Dave has never smoked and tried to ensure that he had a good balanced diet and healthy lifestyle. He was also keen to keep things in our life as normal as possible, continuing with the things we enjoyed like going out or running. He was interested in the science and was present to provide his sperm sample, as well as being there at both embryo transfers. The first is with my eggs and the second is with our egg donor. Dave loved looking at the pictures of the embryos and talking to the embryologists as it made him feel like part of the journey.

When I ask Dave about how he felt during the time I was very unwell, he tells me he felt bad for putting my body through everything and just wanted the old Kate back. Dave found the hardest part was after we had the miscarriage as we were both sad. Although he only went to two counselling sessions, and he didn't say much, he said listening to the counsellor's advice was very helpful. Dave says that he found it hard when some of his close friends had children because he then felt excluded, and it was a reminder of what he couldn't have. Again, we often focus on how women feel when close friends have children, but it is important to be aware that men have these feelings just as much as women but they may not show it.

Fertility Fact
Men the Forgotten or Missing Piece

When we think about fertility treatment or pregnancy loss, we often think about the female partner. This is understandable as in fertility, most of the treatment focuses on the female partner, all the invasive tests, medical procedures and medication. As women, it is us who carry the pregnancy and have the baby. It is women who might experience the physical and medical aspects of a pregnancy loss. However, when we think about it, we need both egg and sperm to make a baby and we often forget about men in this equation.

Busting a myth here and now that infertility is not just a women's issue. Male factor fertility is just as common as female factor fertility. While we associate fertility treatment with women, men are also important. If you have a male partner, he will also need to get their sperm checked and there are other tests also that may be needed as part of the fertility treatment workup – this was discussed in a previous fertility fact.

Men can often feel like a spare part; after all, they have the easy bit – donating sperm at the right time for fertility treatment. They often don't have to go through all the tests and treatment and won't experience the physical symptoms of a miscarriage. But they are also a man wanting to experience parenthood and be a father. We also know that more research is needed to focus on men, fertility and pregnancy loss and needs to include their thoughts, feelings and experiences. There are people out there who are doing a great job researching, sharing their stories and ensuring that there is increased education and support in this area.

Chapter 13

Moving Forward.

I continued nursing in a full-time clinical role, working at the fertility clinic where I had my treatment. After all, I loved the job, had spent many years working towards a specialised role and had my Bourn family who had looked after me – what a privilege! However, the emotions began to take their toll, most aspects of the job were fine with me, but other ones were a struggle. Assisting with embryo transfers was particularly hard; my role was to support the couple and assist the doctor. Having an embryo transfer is like having a smear test, the woman lies down on a couch with her feet in stirrups, the doctor skilfully feeds in a very small flexible catheter through the vagina and cervix, the embryo is attached to the catheter in a small syringe of fluid, this is then transferred to the uterus. Part of the procedure also means the woman has to have a full bladder and we can also perform a trans-abdominal scan, so we can see the catheter entering the cervix and uterus. Before the procedure begins, the patient will talk to the embryologist who will update them on how their embryos have been over the last few days. They can also provide pictures and a video. Once the embryo transfer is done, the patient can go home and is usually given a pregnancy test and a date to test on. This usually takes two weeks, and this time is affectionally referred to as the "two-week wait". The period after an embryo transfer, before you know whether you are pregnant or not, can be particularly challenging. Every time I would assist with a transfer, in my head I would be right back at my transfer, imagining it was me and Dave talking to the embryologists. It was us being handed the pregnancy tests or the embryo pictures. Maybe it was because those were all the pictures we ever had. They were visual evidence of our fertility journey.

One day, I was in the scan room. It had been a busy morning, and my job was to scan all the patients for that day. These patients either needed follicular tracking scans to monitor their response to treatment or a pregnancy scan to confirm if their pregnancy was viable. After this particular day, when I had two patients with pregnancy scans that were not viable, I was again taken back to my treatment, imagining myself sitting in the scan chair just as they were receiving the bad news. I decided then and there that as much as I loved working here, I just couldn't continue any longer. It was time to make a big decision about my future.

I thought that I would play it safe and stay in fertility. It's a niche area to work in and if you have the skills, you can usually find other work elsewhere with other clinics, so this is what I did. It turned out to be a promotion as a nurse manager in another clinic which was about an hour's drive away from home. At first, it seemed like a great idea, a new challenge, a promotion, and a chance to prove myself, something I hadn't been able to do on my fertility journey. Looking back, it was probably one of the worst things I could have ever done. I had no support at work, was in a higher pressured job and was still struggling with many symptoms both from the progesterone hypersensitivity and from POI because at this point, I wasn't yet back on my HRT.

The first few weeks were the honeymoon period, everything was fine and I was settling in, but then things began to change. I couldn't remember things, I struggled to concentrate, I couldn't construct sentences or numbers in my brain and I kept repeating mistakes. I was very honest; I told my managers about what had happened and I also recognised that the symptoms were probably down to both of the conditions. I had recently restarted my HRT, which was helping, but as I tell patients now, it takes time to find the right regime for you. I returned to meet my GP who this time was very helpful and referred me back to the menopause clinic. I told my manager about the plan that I would be meeting a specialist again and would also put a plan in place to help with my work such as other staff members checking my work before I sent it out and allowing more time to complete tasks. I knew that it would be a challenge but this could be a good starting point.

Initially, my employer agreed, but a few days later they asked me to come into the office for a chat. They explained that they thought the role wasn't working and then gave me a letter that invited me to a disciplinary hearing the following day. I was stunned. I was still in my probation period, so I knew that there wasn't much I could do. I drove home in a state of shock and had to pull over on the motorway to be sick. How had it gotten this far? What kind of person was I if I couldn't do my job any more? I got home, ran upstairs to the bathroom still retching. Dave was about to leave for work, but this time he didn't because he saw the state I was in. He pleaded with me to phone the nursing union; I said what good would it do? Once I had calmed down, I phoned the union and explained everything that had happened. The union were brilliant, they said that as I was in my probation period I had very little rights and they couldn't get a representative to attend tomorrow due to the short notice. But if I asked to rearrange the meeting, they would get a representative to attend alongside me. Dave said that he would go with me. My mum even offered to drive down from her house which was a three-hour drive to attend the meeting with me. There and then, I decided to resign. My job has always been a big part of my life, but it was then I realised after everything that it didn't need to be and I could make the right decision for myself. Why put myself through that? I was unwell, struggling with symptoms and was trying my best and I had been honest about it. It was better to put myself first for once.

The following day, I went to work. Dave drove me there and waited in the car so that I wouldn't have to drive home in a state of physical upset. I told my team that I was leaving. Then I handed my notice to my managers. For a long time, I wouldn't talk about leaving a job, it was embarrassing, it was shameful and yet again I had failed. But now when I look back, I am glad that I left. It was the right thing to do. The job wasn't for me, and I knew that there would be other opportunities out there.

I had a few weeks off to get my head around things. I then took a completely different job working for NHS Blood and Transplant, part managing a blood donation team with another colleague. This was the best thing I could have done; I had a complete break from fertility both personally and professionally and got to work with a great colleague. We job-shared for just over two years, fostering a supportive relationship that revitalised my passion and confidence in both nursing and my work colleagues. But over time, I began to realise that I missed working in women's health. I started to do independent work offering fertility consultations, but it wasn't enough. I missed working in a specialty where I had worked for years, built up significant knowledge and felt that it was time to go back.

It was as if fate was watching. My good friend who still worked at my old clinic rang me one day and said, 'Do you want to come back and work with me again but in a different clinic?' My answer was yes. We were like Ying and Yang or Dumb and Dumber as we used to call ourselves as a joke. We had worked together for many years running an egg donation programme and I couldn't wait to be back working in an area I loved with colleagues and friends I knew so well. It also meant that I could continue my independent fertility and menopause work I had begun to slowly build up. I met another great friend who gave me my big break working independently just before I returned to work in fertility. This really opened my eyes, I could use my knowledge to work independently offering consultations, work-based advice and work-based training. I didn't know it yet, but this would be a positive step forward in my work-life balance in the future.

Healthwise, I was still struggling but things were slowly starting to improve. Over time and trial and error, I found the right HRT route and dose. I was also taking antidepressants which had helped with the progesterone side effects including anxiety. I also began to introduce regular mindfulness. With time, as I started to feel better, I began to process and accept what had happened. I was able to learn from the past and be more honest about my condition. I began this process while still working at NHSBT. I was honest with my employer about some of the symptoms I was experiencing, particularly memory problems, difficulty with numbers and brain fog. My new manager was very supportive, giving me extra time to do tasks or ask questions. This was all I needed – time and support. I continued this when I returned to working in fertility; being honest if I couldn't remember something, asking questions and allowing extra time to do tasks. It felt like a weight was lifted from my shoulders. I could be honest without fear it would have a negative impact. I also worked on coping strategies to add to the toolbox such as always having a notebook to write things down, a paper and electronic diary and reaching for mindfulness and breathing exercises during a bad day. I worked in a clinical role in fertility until deciding to change to a new role working in nurse lecturing in 2021.

Could It Have Been Predicted?

This is something I have wondered and something I have also been asked about. Would there be a way that this could have been predicted? This has made me look back on my gynaecological history more closely. I started my periods later in life, around the age of 14, unlike other girls. It was a long-waited symbol of adulthood. I had read the Judie Bloom books that told me about puberty and went to the school nurse talks at school which told me about period products and how not to get pregnant. My friends and fellow students began to start their periods, but I was still waiting. It eventually happened, and I presumed that future periods would be regular and something I could just get on with each month. However, it didn't turn out that way. From the start, my periods were painful, heavy and very irregular. Irregular periods can be common in young girls and is normal in the first two years while the hypothalamic-pituitary-gonadal-axis (HPG) begins to mature. The HPG is responsible for regulating reproductive activity by the release of hormones and associated feedback at certain points in your menstrual cycle. Most young women's periods begin to settle down into a regular pattern after a couple of years. This wasn't the case for me, my periods continued to be a bit of a nightmare. For a few months, they might follow a regular pattern every 26–30 days, then they would be every two weeks, then every 6–8 weeks, or I would bleed continually for weeks at a time. They were heavy, painful and often end up triggering menstrual migraines. It is great being a woman. Like other young women, I tried many options to help manage difficult periods. This ranged from the oral contraceptive pill, progesterone medication, pain relief and medication to reduce the bleeding.

Eventually just before I started my nurse training, they were so bad that I felt like should have shares in Tampax! I had a really embarrassing experience wearing a grey skirt and bleeding on a restaurant chair – you don't forget these experiences! By then, I was in my early twenties, in a long-term relationship and worried about how I would cope working as a student nurse, working a variety of hours, shifts and placements whilst also juggling unpredictable problem periods. I returned to my GP who referred me to gynaecology for further advice. Back then, I was lucky. The waiting list wasn't as long as it is now. I saw a gynaecologist and then had a Mirena coil inserted. While this was quite painful, it was the best thing I could have done. It worked for me and within a few months, my periods stopped altogether. This was so much easier to manage and also acted as a contraception so a great two-for-one.

I had another Mirena coil inserted after the first one ran out (they last up to 5 years). I had the second coil removed in 2012 when in a new relationship with Dave. We began our fertility journey and decided to try to conceive. Even this turned out to be out of the ordinary as when I had the coil removed, they couldn't find it and I had to be referred to the hospital. Luckily, all was well, and I went to the colposcopy clinic which successfully located the coil and removed it. After the coil was removed, it was then I noticed that my periods had changed again. They were still irregular but much lighter and no longer painful. Initially, I had prolonged bleeding, but this then stopped, and I started to have months without a period ranging from 2–11 months when I was tracking my cycle closely.

Looking back, I had used many different types of progesterone over the years to manage my periods ranging from the oral contraceptive pill, the progesterone-only pill, Mirena coil, norethisterone, provera and cyclogest which was used for fertility treatment. I never had any reactions that I was aware of to any of these medication. Whilst I had experienced various symptoms from having problem periods and from taking a variety of hormones, there was nothing I could pinpoint that linked to the severe reaction and symptoms I had experienced during the final IVF cycle in 2017 where I became pregnant and extremely unwell.

I kept thinking and the only experience I could think back to which happened a few years before when I experienced labial swelling and pain for no reason. It happened in between some of our fertility treatments. I wasn't using any hormones or any contraceptives and for a few days, I experienced intense pain and itching in my labial area. I spent the weekend using cream and ice packs, thinking I had thrush or some sort of allergic reaction, even though nothing had changed in my diet or lifestyle. I even visited the out-of-hours GP who asked if I had a sexually transmitted infection, all swabs came back clear which was as I suspected, and after a few days, the symptoms finally cleared when my period started. I put this down to a one-off unusual episode and never thought about it again. Could this be related to the reaction I had in 2017? We will never know and may never have the answer. My menstrual cycle history was certainly unique and unpredictable, and never adhered to a regular pattern. Whilst some patients may be able to look back on their history linking it to the symptoms or condition, this wasn't something I could reliably do when looking back at my own reproductive history.

We also know that for many patients, things can change. We are human after all and we don't always behave predictably. We know that patients can respond differently in each treatment cycle so it would be reasonable to think that things can change over time and the way we respond to medication or physiological changes can also differ for lifetime.

The Life That Could Have Been

I am sure that my thoughts are similar to those of others who have experienced a pregnancy loss – over time, you reflect on the life that could have been. You think that eventually you will stop imagining it, but I can honestly say that even as I type this nearly seven years later this March, I still think about that life that could have been. These thoughts are always around the months of March and October. March because this is when the miscarriage happened and October because this was both the month that would have been my due date and also baby loss awareness month which, from the work point of view, is a busy month raising awareness of this important area. But sometimes, other life events can also trigger these thoughts – anything from Mother's Day to something I hear on the news or even a family event.

Your mind is a funny thing; there is no logic or order to it. You might suddenly think, wow, your child would be this age today, or imagine them starting school or completing a particular milestone. Alternatively, you might just see a picture in your mind of what could have been. Everyone is different in how they remember significant events and losses so there is no right or wrong. For me, over time the thoughts are less than they were but nothing is set in stone. A counsellor I saw once compared grief to a wave on a beach coming in and out and I suspect that this is no different. It can vary as we grow through our lives. One of the hardest things is not having anything to show for your loss such as anything physical or a place to hold the memory. So, for people like me who have experienced a pregnancy loss, it is a personal choice on how they choose to remember the life that could have been.

I can only speak for my own experience, but the life that could have been is always with you, something that you carry in your heart. I have a picture of the embryo that could have been there with me, and not just in the picture. Clinics often allow couples or women to take pictures of the embryo from the lab. A beautiful painting that was painted by a midwife who specialises in embryo and pregnancy art, that stunning blue painting sits on my desk in my office as a visual reminder.

Furry Friends

Dave and I had always been animal lovers. When I first moved to Harwich to live with Dave, Dave had 3 cats named Polar, Zeus and Greebo. I had 23 guinea pigs and a ginger cat called Ted. Over the years, the number of piggies gradually reduced. We lost Greebo and gained another cat from a rescue – Mazie. I was in the hairdresser's one day talking to my lovely hairdresser, who had been cutting my hair for years. I said the words that would change our lives once again. 'We are thinking of getting a dog.'

My hairdresser Sam said, 'There is a great rescue down the road you could try.' I went home and told Dave about that. We went to visit the rescue just to have a look that afternoon. We were introduced to a lovely 16-week-old rescue puppy, a real cutie, and a Heinz 57 mix breed. It was odd as the rescue staff said, 'She had initially had another family inquire about her.' I thought why they were showing that lovely puppy to us. I watched as she perched on Dave's shoulder, a tiny little fluff ball. It turned out that the rescue thought we were a better fit for the cute puppy. We said yes in a heartbeat and adopted her there and then, counted the days until we could collect her.

Dave was so excited. The following week, I was away at a nursing conference, and he kept texting me, *'When will they do the home check? When can we go and pick her up?'* It was like his depression had lifted and he had a new focus. We eventually picked up this wonderful bundle of cuteness took her home and named her Lottie. Lottie was the glue we needed to help us heal. She was cute, kind and a complete character. We then embarked on first time puppy ownership and training. All of a sudden, we didn't feel so alone, and life felt like we had a purpose again. I know I am biased but everyone who meets Lottie seems to love her. All I can say is that it is almost like she was meant to be with us. Our dog addiction began. We then subsequently rescued a lurcher, greyhound and another lurcher, bringing our K9 total to four who we called the Pleace Pack!

Everyone finds their own path and there are different journeys but for us, the dogs gave us a purpose, particularly for Dave. He now had four-legged friends to focus on. It got him out of the house on regular walks and he met more people. One of our lurchers had some behavioural issues so we consulted a dog behaviourist and trainer. This was a big learning experience for us. Dave, in particular, took time to learn about how dogs interact and behave so we could give our dogs the best life possible. He also began a micro business walking a small number of dogs. If you see Dave with any dog, he is like a child who has been given some sweets. He smiles and enjoys petting the dog, chatting with the owner sharing various dog tips and stories. This was a new hobby and emerging area of passion for him. The dogs live a life that we would all want to live; food, regular walks, play time and sleeping on our sofas and beds. This would be the life we would all want for ourselves. We also changed our holidays, stayed more in the UK in dog-friendly cottages so we could holiday with the dogs and explore new places going for long dog walks.

Running for a Positive

I began running around the same time as we started our fertility journey in 2013. I'm not a natural runner, never did sport as a teenager and Dave could walk at my running pace. I started small and slowly worked my way up. I first ran a race for life after my aunt experienced cancer. I decided that it was a great cause to fundraise for and a good challenge for a non-active cake lover like me. A friend offered to help me learn to run, taking me down to the beach weekly for so-called runs, or more like torture. I would moan, say that it hurt. I wanted to stop it but over time, I gradually increased the distance I could run and eventually ran the race for life in 2014. It wasn't quick, it wasn't pretty and it was really hot, but I got to the end, was still alive and fundraised for a great cause.

I decided to carry on running, continuing regular runs. I even joined my local running club – Harwich Runners. I'm not sure if I was the new member they wanted, slower than a snail. I didn't stop talking on my runs or waving at people and always wanted cake at the end. But my mum always said that I ran my race and she was right, that's what I did. The running bug spread to two of my closest friends I had known since school. We all live in different parts of the country and have been friends for over thirty years. We refer to our group as Cobra. We both started running and did a 10K together in Cardiff. No one would have imagined we would have done that years earlier when we were out clubbing or having a drink in the pubs.

The running bug continued alongside our fertility journey. It was a good way to help with the stresses of the journey and was something else to focus on. I slowly improved and completed longer distance runs including a 10-mile run and several half marathons including the Berlin and Amsterdam half marathon. I made some great friends along the way who are still part of my life, and it taught me how important it is to be active. In late 2017, I decided to use my running to help bring our fertility journey to a positive close. I applied to run the London 2018 marathon with the miscarriage association and was accepted to run in their 2018 marathon team. The training began immediately, a plan was devised and several marathon training books were purchased.

I knew that this would be a tough journey. I had never run a marathon. I was a slow runner and I was still juggling a variety of symptoms from POI and progesterone hypersensitivity. However, I had already learnt not all paths are easy. I started the training plan aiming to run three times a week, two short runs in the week or training at a running club and one long run at weekends. One of my good running friends joined me on the longer runs, we chatted and ate jelly babies and her company and support were invaluable. We even went out in the snow. As part of the training, I completed a 10-mile run with Dave the test track 10 miles in the Basildon and the London Land Marks half marathon with running buddies and two other friends. It was great to be out for running and being social. There is a great picture of me wearing a bin bag just before the London Landmarks half marathon looking very stylish but also warm. My last run was a 20-mile training run. My running buddy loved it, smiling all the way round. By 18 miles, I was grumbling to myself, counting every step but we got there. I went home, collapsed in the chair and demanded Dave to cook me food. I was marathon-ready.

The miles were slowly increasing each week, and I then had to focus on fundraising. This was such an important cause, something that had happened to me and happened to many other women and impacted many people's lives. Team Kate got stuck in. My mum made a beautiful quilt which we raffled off. She also made bunting and craft decorations which we sold at craft stalls. We had a permanent cake stall at the fertility clinic with a donation box, that was very popular with my workmates and me. Another friend ran the Colchester marathon and did a work cooking day. The running club did a breakfast run. My running buddy even organised a party in the evening where we all danced the night away to raise money, now that was a great night! Donations poured in from friends, family and generous people, some of whom I had never met. By the time April marathon month arrived, we were over target; all I had to do was actually run the marathon.

Marathon day finally arrived. Dave and my mum were my support crew and my sister did a Facebook takeover updating everyone else. In true style, the challenge escalated; marathon day was the hottest day on record for the London Marathon. I had no choice but to get stuck in. I hated the heat, but decided to take it mile by mile. I had my hat, my jelly babies, I could do this! I set off, and by the time my start wave went it was after 11, this would be a long day! I took it mile by mile, and each mile on the course was marked with red balloons. The support was amazing, with members of the public cheering and watching, bands, singers, you name it. I saw Dave and my mum several times around the course which was nice. Although the heat was a challenge, my phone died in the heat and when I met Mum and Dave by the tower bridge, I had run rage. My mum offered me an ice cream, but that was not what I wanted. I remember throwing my phone at poor Dave saying it wouldn't work. Then realising as I was at Tower Bridge that I still had 13 miles to run as that is roughly halfway round!

I kept running, I met up with other miscarriage association teammates. I remember it being so hot it felt like heat was rising up from the concrete. I walked for miles it was so hot. By this point, those at the back of the pack were getting to the water stations and there was no water. Luckily, the good people of London did not disappoint. People went into their houses, returning with tubs of water for runners. We were so grateful! I could see dozens of runners being taken into medical tents. I didn't want this to be me, as that might mean I would have to run it again. I kept walking for another hour or so until it started to cool. I could then regroup and hopefully start running again. When you are a slower runner, you usually end up with a group of runners who you see regularly throughout the course. They are usually running a similar pace to you. You may pass them and when you stop or slow down, they may pass you. For me, it was two guys dressed as Rhinos. I would say as they passed by, 'Hello again, Rhino.'

As the day began to turn to evening. I was still running. Would this ever end? There were even supporters handing out sandwiches now. If I stopped to eat one, I doubted I would be able to get moving again. I continued run / walking eventually making it to the embankment. You know you are not far then as you can see the river and the houses of parliament. This was when I saw Dave. He is easy to spot because he is so tall. This was the only time I got emotional and the end was in sight. Could I get there? I stopped briefly but the school teacher inside my head said, 'You have to finish this, now get going.' I then saw signs for 400 yards nearly there (no, that was the longest 400 yards of my life). Then 200 yards, then there it was the finish line.

By the time I finished, the crowd had died down. I could spot my support crew and a lovely volunteer gave me my medal. I had done it. My mum's first words were priceless: "Thank goodness, you're still alive." My thought was that I had made it and wouldn't have to do it again. Dave and I had booked the hotel for that evening as I didn't want to hobble back home on the train. We had a meal out. I refused to take off my medal, then I hobbled back to the hotel room round the corner instead. I had finished my first marathon and had fundraised for a brilliant cause that could make a difference to other people who were experiencing pregnancy loss. Once we made it home the following day, I went with the other Harwich runners to the running club that week for a photo for the local paper. I had done it; I had run the London Marathon!

Fertility Fact

The Miscarriage Association. Why They Matter

Around 1 in 4 couples may experience a miscarriage. It often isn't spoken about and is one of the last healthcare taboos. The chances are that you may have a family member or friend who has been through it, and you may not even know because not everyone talks about it. A pregnancy loss can happen at any stage of the pregnancy. For us, it was in early pregnancy during the first few weeks. We were open with our experience and story but many others wanted to know that they were not alone and others were there who may have experienced something similar. This was when I reached out to the miscarriage association. Just reading the information on their website and knowing that I wasn't alone was a great comfort during a difficult time.

The Miscarriage Association is a charity that was founded in 1982. The charity supports patients and couples who have had a miscarriage or pregnancy loss. They provide information, have a support line that you may call and run support groups. They even help to shape miscarriage and pregnancy loss policies at the policy level. They have resources and information for workplaces and health care professionals on their website and highlight current research in this area. They have a shop where you can buy cards to send to loved ones who have a miscarriage. They are a small charity with a small and committed team who were there for us on marathon day, cheering us on offering us oranges and supporting us all the way to the finish line.

There are lots of ways to support this great cause which offers a lifeline of support during a difficult journey. This could be from making a donation, volunteering or even putting yourself up for a challenge to raise funds. It doesn't have to be a marathon, there are lots of different challenges to choose from. You can find out more on their website www.miscarriageassociation.org.uk.

There's No Time for Us (Queen)
Time is a funny thing; sometimes, it goes by really quickly, and other times, it doesn't. Time can mean different things to different people. When I think of you, looking back we didn't have much time together, you and I, barely a few weeks at most. Much of that time was spent in a state of anxiety, pain, feeling ill, severely sleep deprived and trying to think of anything else both medically and physically that I should be doing to help solve this puzzle of hell I was now living in. Secretly, I was saying in my head to you to just hang on, not to give up, even if it seemed like my body was trying to.

It wasn't how I imagined being pregnant would be. Yes, I

imagined that there would be symptoms, all the things I had seen my family, friends and patients have; such as fatigue, nausea, stomach pains, sickness and hormone changes. But nothing to the extent that I was experiencing. Nothing that had turned both my body and mind into a raging monster. Nothing that had made me scream at Dave many times, 'I feel like I am dying, or I feel like I am burning, on fire on the inside.'

The time you and I had together was a rollercoaster. We never had time to sit and be you and me. A mother and her unborn baby, bonding from the inside, me giving you a safe home until you were ready to meet the world. It just didn't happen. Time was something we never had; no time to plan, no time to meet you at a long-awaited scan appointment, no time to shop for baby clothes, no time to imagine what you were getting up to on the inside. No time for you, me and Dave to be together, just us three. The rollercoaster was suddenly over, just as quickly as it had started.

It was me who stopped the watch; I had stopped our time in its tracks. I knew that once I stopped taking the progesterone support medication, the chances of the pregnancy would become extremely small. Yet, I had still decided to make time stop and stand still. Time stood still and your time ended because I could no longer fight the good fight. The pendulum had swung in the other direction, and I could no longer cope with the symptoms and feeling so unwell. It didn't mean that I wouldn't hope for a miracle. I still hoped that you would hang on, you would beat the odds. But it just wasn't to be. The odds were stacked against you and were not something you or I could beat at that time.

Time goes on and I still think of you often, as I'm sure others do who have experienced a pregnancy loss. Sometimes, I wonder what you might have become, or what milestone you might have reached. Sometimes, I'm sad when I think of you; other times, I wish I had just a few minutes with you so that I could explain how I had tried but couldn't hold on any longer. How it was the hardest decision I had ever had to make, and how sorry I was. How time had been against us. There were other times when I thought of you and wanted you to know that you are never forgotten. I wanted to tell you about my new path, and how you might not be here, but you were helping others. Time may have stopped for us, but hopefully, it wouldn't stop for other people.

In time, I also commissioned an artist with a specialist interest in reproductive art to paint a picture of you. For most pregnancies that are lost in the early weeks, there often isn't a visual record of the pregnancy. But for you, that was different; because we had IVF, we had your embryo picture that was taken on the day of our embryo transfer. It was beautiful! You were beautiful and the picture that the artist painted of you will always be beautiful and always with us. For those students and patients that I often have online meetings or consultations with, they might see you in the corner of the camera as you sit with me on my desk in my little office. You are the pride of the place and part of all the work I am now privileged to do in women's health. You are seen, you are there.

Time has also given individuals who have experienced pregnancy loss the option of recognition. Thanks to some tireless and great work from a small group of determined individuals, if you like me have experienced a pregnancy loss, you can now apply for a pregnancy loss certificate that acknowledges and recognises your pregnancy loss. I'm not eligible to apply for a certificate because it's only for those who have experienced a pregnancy loss after 2018 (mine happened in 2017). However, once I am able, I will also apply for your certificate, acknowledgment and official recognition.

Fertility Fact
What Is the Impact of Stopping the Progesterone Support

Medication?

As I already said previously, the hormone progesterone plays an important part in supporting an early pregnancy until the placenta begins to develop and take over producing the hormones needed to support and continue the pregnancy. For most people who conceive naturally, the corpus luteum produces the hormone progesterone after ovulation and will continue to do so for those early few weeks of pregnancy.

For me, because I had IVF treatment using a donor egg, it meant that my body was not likely to produce any of the hormones needed to support the pregnancy naturally. Before starting the treatment, I had extremely irregular periods and they had virtually stopped altogether, so it would be extremely unlikely that my ovaries would be producing any of the hormones needed to help support the pregnancy until the placenta took over.

Therefore, I would be relying on the hormones that I was taking to support the pregnancy (oestrogen and progesterone medication) until the placenta would be able to take over producing the hormones. Stopping the medication would potentially leave me and the baby without any hormones supporting the pregnancy. The pregnancy may continue but without these crucial hormones, the chances of an ongoing pregnancy were extremely slim.

Chapter 14

The Future

It is hard to accept a path that you did not choose or want to follow. You feel like everyone is on another path, moving ahead with expected and accepted life changes whilst you either swim in circles or decide to follow a new path. For a long time, I wasn't sure what to do, it felt like I was just wandering through life a week or day at a time. That's not necessarily a bad thing. It was a change of thinking that was very helpful for me. When you are on a fertility journey, you are constantly looking ahead to the next appointment, scan or treatment cycle, waiting for the expected path. Living more day-to-day educated my mind in a new way. I would only think about what I was doing the next day rather than weeks or months ahead.

I went through a rollercoaster of feelings; this hasn't changed much over the years but is much more dialled down than it used to be a bit like the volume button on your car. Over time, the volume has been turned down, but it doesn't mean that it can't be turned up again. I felt that people would be judging and looking at me, thinking, well, what is her life for if she isn't having children? I felt that I would have to work twice as hard for recognition because having a child guarantees that next step of approval in society. What could I possibly offer if there was no baby? Nothing to talk about at family gatherings, no birthday parties or school pictures. How could I ever say my life was hard if I wasn't a parent? I wasn't responsible for anyone else and had no commitments. I couldn't be tired as I would always have a good night's sleep without anyone waking me up. Moreover, I didn't have to do the nursery or school run. My life was a one-way ticket to paradise with no commitments, plenty of sleep and the chance to go on holiday at the drop of a hat. At least that's what outsiders may think.

However, no one tells you how isolating and lonely it can be. You watch your friends have children. They might become more distant as their new life shapes around their children and your life remains the same. They may seem understandably pre-occupied with their new family life, or constantly invite you to birthday parties and gatherings while you just crave some adult time with a friend who is willing to be present and listen. You may find that you are surrounded by a lot of triggers. This could be pregnancy announcements, children's birthday parties, social media and neighbours to name a few. You may be like me in the first few years and not feel confident to say no. Society expects you to go, it's your friend, they have a baby and they would like to see you at the party. You often put your own feelings aside and think to see the bigger picture; it's only a few hours, I can cope.

But putting your feelings aside and just coping can be like a mini assault course, navigating those few hours, wondering what to do or say, how you can get away with leaving early or standing in the corner. When you get the courage to go to a friend's baby party, you may then be surrounded by parents who may mean well, but often the conversation is dominated by pregnancy, children and their activities. It takes time and courage to be able to sit back, disconnect and decide which, what or where you want to go with your new path. For me, my path wasn't an immediate light bulb moment. It emerged over several months as time went on.

Why Don't You Just Adopt?

This is a good and very relevant question and often what most people expect to happen if you can't have children, or if you have tried various fertility treatments which weren't successful. I have been asked this question many times and at different times in my fertility journey and the answer is always yes, we did think about adoption. Having a family was very important to us and we thought long and hard about adoption. We also looked into this possibility very closely, contacting our local authority for more information and speaking to others who have gone down this path. However, for us, we made a very personal decision that adoption wasn't the right path for us. Adoption is a very personal choice; these are very special children who need the right family and home, and adoption should not be seen as a substitute path. Adoption is not an easy path; it has a lengthy application stage which can take months or even years and the path is unknown once you adopt. For many people, adoption is the right path they go on to give that child or children a home and it completes their family.

If you are thinking of adopting, know that this is an amazing thing to do that potentially could change the lives of you and the child or children you adopt. Find out all the information you can on adoption and the process, also speak to others who have travelled the same path who can provide invaluable information and personal experience. Finally, know that adoption isn't necessarily a prerequisite if your fertility treatment hasn't been successful. For us, completing our family was more on the four-legged friends' side. With the adoption of our four rescue dogs over the last few years, the house will never be the same again, but having dogs was the right path for us.

Fertility Fact

Not All Fertility Treatment Ends with a Baby

This is something that we don't talk about enough. When we think about fertility treatment, what do we see in the media? We see the success stories, the baby at the end and not giving up. It will happen if you just try hard enough. It's great to celebrate the positive as it can have a significant impact on people's lives and their journey through parenthood. We see celebrities having children at older ages or who may choose to use a surrogate. What we don't see is that, in real life, many cycles don't end with a baby and that fertility treatments often don't work.

The numbers don't lie and trust me, I don't do numbers. We know that success rates on an IVF cycle can vary but are typically around 35% (HFEA). This means many cycles don't end with a baby. IVF does not guarantee a pregnancy or a baby and the decision to end fertility treatment is a personal choice. No one wants to hear about what happens when treatment doesn't work or from those who have made the personal and heart-breaking decision to end treatment. This should not be seen as giving up, but as being brave enough to accept a new path. This is something that we need to change, the narrative on more IVF cycles. Sadly, not working for those who do, it is a must that these stories and individual voices are heard, recognised and supported.

You Can Always Try Again

For many people who have experienced a pregnancy loss, this is something others often say to you. Often because no one ever really knows what to say to someone who has lost a baby. It is human nature for people to want to say something positive to you, so this is often the first thing that is said, 'Don't worry, you can always try again.' After all, it sounds so reassuring, so positive and caring. For some individuals and couples, it's also true, they can try again when they are ready if they are trying to conceive naturally, or although there are no guarantees, think about another cycle of fertility treatment.

For us, it became clear that it wasn't an option. While trying

123

naturally was possible, it was extremely unlikely and as I have mentioned earlier. Although possible, the chances of conceiving naturally with POI are low around 5%. Having an IVF with my eggs offered a low chance and having an IVF using egg donation still offered the best chances of success which as before were between 30–40%. This meant that like many others, if we wanted to try again, we would have to consider IVF using egg donation, which was both costly and time-consuming.

Due to what had happened in the previous cycle and the subsequent diagnosis of severe progesterone sensitivity, a future pregnancy now seemed extremely difficult and risky, whether through natural conception or IVF treatment using egg donation. If we wanted to try again, we would have to navigate both IVF using egg donation and an uncharted treatment plan aimed at treating the progesterone sensitivity, a plan that was also high risk and offered no guarantee of working.

The high-risk plan would have involved trial cycles using progesterone and a combination of steroids and antihistamines which would dampen down my immune system and help treat and reduce the symptoms. The plan would be that if future fertility treatment worked and I became pregnant, the aim would be to take the progesterone support only for the minimum amount of time possible, with the goal of stopping the progesterone medication as soon as is safe to do so once the placenta had started to develop and take over the function of supporting the pregnancy.

We spent a lot of time thinking about our options and eventually made the difficult decision that this would be the end of our fertility journey and we would not be going ahead with any further fertility treatment. We had reached the end of the road for us and felt that although our hand was forced, we had made the right decision for us.

Whilst I understand why people would say to me those seven dreaded words 'Don't worry, you can always try again' and my reaction used to be to smile and nod, but from the inside, I wanted to scream, "No, I can't try again, it's not as simple as that. It's complex, it's risky and I might lose another baby or even my life this time." But I never told anyone that, I would usually just wait for the moment to pass or would delicately change the subject. Should I have been honest and said something? Maybe. But you can't go back in time, and back then I just didn't feel comfortable sharing and also doubted it would be something everyone would be ready to hear or listen to.

If You Really Want It, Don't Give Up

This is also something that has stayed in my head both now and throughout our fertility journey. Often people would advise me not to give up, try everything and try harder. I knew they meant no harm and wanted to say something that would help during an uncomfortable silence or conversation. I would see quotes on social media saying keep going, it will happen. If you really want it, you will do everything you can and you will achieve your dream of motherhood. This circled in my mind: Had I done everything? Had I tried hard enough? Did people think I should have done more? I would have conversations with Dave, questioning if I could have done more. He would always reassure me that I was very ill and had done all I could, but it didn't always make me feel better. Our society expects that if we work hard enough, we will achieve everything we want in life and all our goals, and in some cases, it is true if you are in the workplace completing a project or studying for a course. However, this isn't always the case when it comes to our health or fertility.

Despite all the changes in technology and new treatments, we do not have all the answers in medicine or the cure for every disease or illness, and sometimes you have to accept that you tried everything you could but at some point, you have to decide that despite trying everything, this is not a path you can stay on. This is no means an easy decision to make, and this was no different for us. We did not jump to a decision to stop everything, we had many conversations with advice from specialists before we made our final decision to end our fertility journey. Often, we don't hear from or know other people who have walked this path. No one wants to talk about going through a journey of a rollercoaster of emotions, injections, medical procedures, hormonal changes and illness that didn't lead to a baby. This is not the success story the media likes to publish but it is a powerful story that should be heard.

Is There Anyone Else Out There?

One of the important things I regularly say to my patients is to reach out and seek support. Find your tribe, a group that gets you or has been through a similar experience. They can be a wonderful source of support, a listening post. There is something powerful about sharing your story or experiences to help others. A support group can help you feel less lonely, and many studies have shown since the 1980s the benefits of a support group demonstrating their effectiveness and their positive outcomes. Support groups can decrease anxiety, improve patient perceptions of their condition and help to educate family and friends. People who receive good support in the presence of challenging situations have better adaptation and have the opportunity to improve coping strategies.

Whilst I have seen many patients impacted by different

forms of progesterone sensitivity, this has generally been in the context of patients using hormone therapy such as HRT or other types of contraception. Patients did experience a variety of symptoms, but there was nothing about the type of symptoms I had experienced. When I asked experienced clinicians and nurses, they also agreed that this was something that they hadn't seen before. At the time of writing, I had never met or heard of a patient who had gone through a similar experience to mine.

This doesn't mean that patients are not out there. When I looked at the research and clinical studies, some patients experienced severe symptoms like mine in relation to the hormone progesterone. However, this was rare, with an extremely small number of patients recorded as having these symptoms. The articles I looked at had only a small number of patients and were from a various countries around the world.

Currently, there are no specific support groups for progesterone sensitivity, and as it is a rare condition impacting a small number of women, there may not be a demand to set up a support group for patients. However, since the COVID-19 outbreak, this has shown us how we can work and live in a different way, making the world a much smaller place and using technology to our advantage. So, maybe in the future, a support group could be started online so that it could be accessible to women across the world even if there are only small number of patients impacted. If you are reading this and you are a patient who has suffered something similar, don't hesitate to get in touch, you are not alone.

Maybe My Body Just Doesn't Do Pregnancy

It is hard after a journey where you lost your fertility, a pregnancy and nearly your life to look at your body in the same way. You look at yourself in the mirror and don't feel like the same person you were before the journey started. Although it's still you with the same flaws, something has changed. You just don't feel like the old you; you are different in some way. It's hard to see yourself in the same light after such a significant journey and life-changing experience. You look at yourself in a different light, things are different and there is a new norm. For me, I felt that my body had failed at the major life hurdle that most women manage to get past. I was able to accept over time that it would be extremely unlikely that I would ever genetically be able to have a child of my own due to having POI. But I had always thought that there would be a good chance of being pregnant and having a child using a donor egg. I had seen many patients at the clinic where I work with POI who had gone on to have egg donation and have children and a family of their own. I had seen the joy in those patients' eyes of finally having a baby.

Now for me, this wasn't going to be the case. Even being pregnant was extremely high risk and would need a specialist plan. There would be no guarantee that things would be any better if I tried again. In fact, they could be much worse. Maybe I wouldn't be able to come out in one piece if we tried again. We had made the decision not to try again, there were too many risks. This didn't mean that it was a decision we had wanted to make. The decision was not easy and had taken time. We went through all the options and made the right decision for us. It didn't mean that life went back to normal and I felt the same as before the journey started. This was simply not the case. Now when I looked in the mirror, I saw someone different, someone who hadn't got past that life-changing hurdle that all women were expected to jump over. My body wasn't able to do what other women's bodies were able to do, I was a reproductive failure. I would always be different – a childless woman, surrounded by mystery, not following the same expected life path. I felt for a long time that my body had let me down not once but twice: first, by not being able to use my genetics, and second, by not being compatible with pregnancy – a double hit!

It was an invisible grief; this wasn't something many people understood or wanted to talk about. Our story was wrapped up in so many taboos, failed fertility treatment, premature menopause, suffering a pregnancy loss, not being able to be a biological mother and not being able to be pregnant. Hardly a conversation starter or subject that people would want to talk about. There was also the guilt of moving on. My baby had not survived because I couldn't tolerate the hormone progesterone or the progesterone medication, yet I had and here I was trying to move on.

Instead for a long time, I didn't talk about it. Over time, I spoke to close friends and family but there was still a lot I have never discussed. The feelings, experiences and not being able to move forward. Although I went to counselling which was very helpful, I didn't go to many support groups, partly because of knowing and understanding the process because I worked in the same area and also because I just didn't want to take the step. Looking back, I wonder if this was something I should have done and shared my story and experience with others who were walking a similar path. Sadly, this is something that I am not able to change.

Is time a healer? Sometimes, the more time passes, the easier some things become, but grief, I find, is a bit like a wave; some days are good and some days are not so good. I think over time, the waves are less strong, but they are still there. Most of the time, the waves are under control, but some days, there might be a trigger or a stressful day that might trigger a storm, more waves coming in and a change in how I may be feeling. A great example is last week when I logged onto a Zoom work call and some staff were showing the team their new babies – lovely but also extremely triggering. Because it was unexpected, I felt quite triggered and unnerved. However, working on my PhD has also helped because I have seen from my research that whilst the situation may not be the same, I am not the only one who felt like this. In my reading into women's experiences of POI, I read several articles that talked about embodiment; how people viewed their bodies, particularly in terms of illness. Of women with POI, some of them also shared a similar view, that their body had changed or had let them down, I wasn't alone in this feeling.

Have I made friends with my body? I am not sure; I think, over time, it has been more of an acceptance. I have accepted what has happened and that it is not something I can change. No matter how hard I try or relax my body, it is not something that I am able to control. My body and mind are no longer the same, they have changed and this is a new norm. All I can do is learn and move forward on a new path, focusing on a new journey and the positive. The positive is that I can move forward even if it is just one small step at a time.

Finding a New Path

"You are considered less than, so you have to be better than to be considered equal." – David Grant (2023)

I always loved working in women's health, and this has been my focus since I first qualified as a nurse way back in 2007. Even before I qualified as a nurse, I knew that I wanted to work in women's health. In my nurse training, I spent my final long placement, known as the management placement, working on a gynaecology ward. I then worked in gynaecology once I finished my training, early pregnancy and then fertility. After the fertility journey ended, it gave me the motivation to focus on a new path in a little more detail. There were a few things I started to juggle with on this unexpected new life path. The first was accepting I would now be living a new life without children, something I discussed in the previous chapter. This is not a path everyone wants or chooses to talk about, but it is so important that women moving on this path are heard. Often invisible or at the back, we are women who are out there, women who are at work, women who are at your children's party with a pang in their hearts, women quietly moving on and living their lives and to all those women, I am that women and I see you!

If you find yourself on this path, the path no one wants to be on, the club no one wants to be in, know that there are others who do see you and know your worth. Know that it is a journey that is different for all of us and that can take time. Don't be afraid to seek support, there are some great support and resources out there such as the Dovecoate support group and Gateway Women, reach out and come out of the shadows when you are ready. This path becomes a part of you; you don't forget your experiences or that you are now walking a path you did not choose. However, over time, you make that path your own, choosing things and experiences that become a part of you.

I decided on the work front that I would walk a new path with a greater focus on women's health, but in a different way. I had always worked and enjoyed my clinical role in fertility, working in a clinic supporting patients on their fertility journey, learning new advanced skills and working with a great team. I decided that it was the time to move forward and branch out so that I could share my knowledge, learn more and be an asset to my patients.

Hello from the Other Side, I'm a Woman Not Just a Womb!

Society is entrenched with traditional paths we feel we should be following. These are set paths in our culture and can be: getting married, having children or going out to work. But what happens when you stray from the path or the path gets taken away? The grief of infertility, pregnancy loss and being childless is often invisible, you have no yearly birthday to remember, grave to visit and often others struggle to understand what that loss is and looks like. It is a lot like physician and mental health, no one has a problem if they see you with a broken leg, this is visible and accepted; however, mental health like grief is invisible, you can't see it and you don't always know that it is there or what the treatment is. This grief is often about what you could have had, the pregnancy you should have experienced, the child you could have and what comes with that; birthdays, school and life events, this has all been taken away from you without anyone even realising.

I can only comment on my own experience but often I feel that I was a failure, less of a person underserving and not a woman. After all, the paths led me to believe a key part of being a woman is having children, something my body wasn't able to do both genetically using my eggs or using a donor's eggs. No one would notice that if I were in a room with other women, I would just feel invisible, useless and my opinion would be irrelevant. After all, I wasn't a parent, how could I ever understand a mother's path? How could I offer something or a contribution to society in any way when my body had failed me so much? At times, these thoughts would often be detrimental to me. I feel I should work twice as hard as those who have children, as my life didn't have that pre-determined path that those with children have mapped out, parenting, the path of raising children. So, at times, I do have a habit of overcommitting particularly on work tasks and opportunities. I find it difficult to say no because of that fear that my life won't matter or be relevant because I am not following that same path. I guess, this is something I have to learn to live with, and going forward, my plan is to look at ways of working with these feelings, developing strategies so that I don't keep overcommitting myself with tasks.

Over the years, I have encountered countless inappropriate comments and well-known cliches, such as 'Just adopt', 'You can always try again', 'Just relax, it will happen', 'My friend went on holiday and got pregnant', 'Does it even matter?' and 'Wow, you must get so much sleep!' Also, there were also some gut-wrenching ones: 'Well, if you don't have children, how will your life ever be enriched?', 'You couldn't possibly understand how hard life is until you are a parent', 'What will you live for now?' I think a big part of it is that no one really knows what to say and not everyone has that awareness and empathy of what it is like being on the other side.

Jodie Day, founder of Gateway Women, estimates that around 1.5 million women in the UK aged in their 40s and 50s are childless, with around only 10% percent choosing to be childfree and a further 10% who are childless due to infertility or medical reasons. Leaving around 80% who are childless by circumstance.

The childless women or men are often invisible, working, paying taxes, looking after parents or just getting on with things. We work extra hours so that people with families can request that time off for school concerts or events. We are at the back in family gatherings, parties, outside of baby sections in supermarkets. One of the things I struggled with was the thought of a legacy. For those with children, that is the legacy you leave: your children and a future path, both in terms of genetics and as someone to preserve your story in the family memories. This wasn't something that would happen for Dave and me, so did not having children mean no legacy? I have thought about this for some time and often struggled with the thought of not leaving a legacy. Then I began to think if leaving a legacy would matter or not. 'Is a legacy just about after you leave this planet?' or 'Does a legacy only apply if you have children; something to pass on to them so that they will tell your story in years gone by?' Then it finally hit me; your legacy isn't having something to pass down to your children, legacy is looking at yourself in the mirror each day and asking the questions if you did everything you planned to, or you went through life in the direction of your moral compass. I talked about legacy on one of the fertility podcast episodes which was about not having children. It was a proud moment being able to chat about this important subject and raise awareness so that others in a similar situation did not feel so alone.

We are possibly the last taboo in employment, often being expected to pick up the work whilst parents are tending to their children or working the hours no one wants to work such as holidays and Christmas, as what these holidays are for if you don't have a family. Society, understandably, is geared and focused on families, schools, events and policies which doesn't always help, as this can make us even more invisible. For a long time, I even felt guilty living in our three-bedroom house. We had bought it just before we started our IVF treatment with the goal of it being our family home, now that wouldn't be the case and yet here we were, taking up space and living in a three-bedroom house that would be ideal for a family, just not ours. Don't panic.

I didn't reach for the estate agents' number; we both really like the house we live in and the area. Instead, I made the little room that would have been the nursery into my work office. It now has a desk, book shelves, a reading chair, lots of artwork and fertility props around the room. There is even a menopause rally sign and a giant sperm! Our other bedroom became the guest room for visitors who are always welcome unless the dogs are sleeping on the bed.

These feelings are still part of me; however, as I type, like other feelings, these are more dialled down. I still often think what my legacy will be. Recently, I read a good article that talked about how if you look back on your family tree, do you remember what your great-great-grandmother did? I certainly didn't; therefore, when thinking about your legacy, it can be anything that you choose or make it to be. I suddenly had this light bulb moment; it wasn't about who might visit me when I am older or who may be at my funeral, it was about me and what I wanted my legacy to be. If it was my last night on earth, when I looked in the mirror, would my legacy look back at me and would it be the impact I had wanted? This change of thought might have happened at this point because I am more accepting of my new path and because I now have a different purpose. It also helps that there are gradually more people like me who are being seen and acknowledged by the public and the media. We then feel visible with more men and women choosing not to have children or who may be childless not by choice. This acknowledges that we are an important group of people who are growing in numbers, who need to be seen and have our stories heard.

My first step on the new path was to return to education. I started a post-graduate diploma in reproductive medicine which I studied on a part-time basis whilst working. I loved soaking up the knowledge, it was so relevant to my area of practice. I then decided to do two years of the MSc; however, a few weeks in it was all too much; panic and lack of confidence got the better of me. I wasn't ready for a statistics module; way too many numbers and dots on graphs that I simply did not understand. I withdrew from the course and carried on working in a clinical role in fertility and at NHSBT. But I didn't give up. Like an itch that I needed to scratch, I returned the following year, and by then symptoms were more under control and I felt more stable to give it another go. I enrolled in the final year and completed the MSc in August 2020. This was the right year, not because of COVID and lockdown but because things just felt better in my mind, and I felt ready. I hate numbers but somehow survived the research and statistics module. Then I also got to write a really interesting MSc thesis on the history of egg freezing, which was both a challenge and a joy to write. The thesis covered how egg freezing has changed since it was first used, predominantly for medical reasons, the increase in social egg freezing and the future implications for women. My good embryologist friend and my mum were the designated proofreaders. They did a fantastic job proofreading and helping me edit it. My mum still says years later she learnt so much from reading it, including that an egg is known as an oocyte. It's never too late to learn; every day is a school day!

I finished and graduated in MSc with distinction in reproductive medicine. The course was extremely relevant to my practice. I had learnt so much and my confidence had increased. Like the marathon, I got through it and made it to the end. I remember logging on to check my grades and feedback, thinking, *Please, just let me make it through.* When I looked at the grades,

I was amazed to see it was a distinction with the suggestion to publish the project I had written on egg freezing. How did I manage to write something that could be considered being published with my remaining one brain cell? High on the wave of finishing, I then had another idea – how about a PhD? It sounds complete madness as I type but that's what my brain was thinking. I saw a great Instagram page of an institution called the Centre for Reproductive Research, which is part of De Montfort University. They were a group of wonderful people who were just like me, they had a passion for women's health and reproductive research. It was like I had come home. They helped me flesh out the idea of a PhD; what it would look like, how it would work and what topic I would choose. I kept going and went ahead with an interview and was offered a part-time PhD that started in January 2021 for my chosen topic – Women's Lived Experience of Premature Ovarian Insufficiency (POI).

I always wanted to do a project or more research on POI, it was an area that was personal to me. I had worked in that area for many years, and I had also supported many patients with POI. I was interested some years ago before my own diagnosis and fertility journey when I began working on an egg donation programme at the clinic. An egg donation programme is usually run by staff at the clinic, including nurses. We help to manage the waiting list for donor eggs and co-ordinate the tests and treatment required for both donors and recipients. One of the things I noticed was that there were several younger patients with POI who were on the waiting list for egg donation. When I spoke to these women, they had usually got funding from the NHS for egg donation treatment and were taking hormone therapy for their menopause symptoms; however, for many, they talked about what a lonely experience it was. Many hadn't seen a specialist for many years, knew no one else with the condition and didn't receive much support.

I kept this with me in a box in my mind for many years, not forgetting the conversations I had with these amazing women, their experiences and their journeys. After conversations with my new team of PhD supervisors, I realised I could focus my research on the subject, 'What did women feel and experience following a diagnosis of POI?' I could listen to women's stories about their journey, their thoughts, feelings and experiences. I could help these women be heard so we could find out more about their journey. So, my PhD journey began. It's a slow start when you are part-time as it can take up to seven years to complete it. In year one, I undertook a development needs analysis, a literature review and started to flesh out what research method I would use. I am now in year two, of my part time PhD and it's starting to ramp up with ethics applications, project reviews and even presenting a poster at a conference. I am hoping the PhD path will continue and can't wait to interview women about their experiences of POI.

Academia does not come naturally to me. In nursing, you are always looking at plan B, then plan C, D, F, H or the grey area. Working and studying academia is very different, it is a whole new way of writing and attention to detail which I am learning slowly. I still don't understand a lot of it, don't like attention to detail or using big words I can't pronounce. But I look at it with great enthusiasm, creativity and hope that I will learn all those other needed skills of creative and analytical writing and attention to detail. Some days, I read research articles and genuinely think I have no idea what that means or how it is relevant to my area of research. But each week, I learn a bit more or tick something else off the to-do list, with each small step getting closer. It is definitely a marathon and not a sprint, which I have learnt more about in the last few weeks, making sure I can manage my time juggling work, study and fitting in a holiday. I'm still on the PhD path hoping to make it to the end.

A Gentle and Passionate Educator

Over time, I also began to do more in the fertility and menopause space. After completing the courses at university, I felt I had the knowledge to begin to support and educate women. This began because of the journey I had been through; I had finally decided to be brave and share my story for the first time in 2020 as I worried that if there was someone else out there going through the same experience, how could they find help? I decided to talk to the fertility podcast. I was familiar with them because I had done a recording with them about the fertility clinic I worked for a few years ago, prior to starting fertility treatment. I found Natalie very easy to talk to and liked her work on the podcast and thought that it would be the right place to share my story. I contacted the podcast and Natalie and her co-host Kate got back to me and we arranged to do a recording of my story.

Whilst making this recording, I started chatting to co-host Kate about the independent work she did in fertility. It sounded empowering and interesting and a way to help patients outside of a fertility clinic. Kate and I chatted for ages and subsequently, I began working with Kate, offering independent fertility consultations. This then branched out over time to include menopause consultations, work-based training and webinars. We are still working together as I type, sharing a great working relationship and friendship.

As my confidence grew, I began to work independently on my own doing menopause talks, work training and educating women and employers on menopause, fertility and POI. I loved talking to women and helping them learn about menopause in a friendly and humorous way, chatting about how amazing our reproductive system is as women, what happens to our periods and why we might experience menopause symptoms. I bust the myths about menopause and HRT, spend time answering their questions and signposting women to different sources of support. My goal is that women won't feel alone like I did and know that there is support and evidence-based information out there.

I'm not great at advertising my independent role, it's not something they teach you when you train to be a nurse – marketing. But over the years, I have slowly been getting busier. I have been to all sorts of places from a garden centre to a science park. It's not quite what the celebrities do but I love it as I get to meet every day awesome women and can have an impact on their lives. I even plucked up the courage to talk on the radio twice. I have also been able to write a couple of articles on egg freezing, progesterone sensitivity and POI that were published in a key women's health magazine rather than a journal so we could get the message out to more healthcare professionals. It's so rewarding to know the message is finally getting out there slowly but surely. I moved to work in a lecturing role at women's health, this is a temporary role that I enjoy as I teach nurses who want to specialise in women's health, helping future nurses support their patients. I will talk to anyone who wants to listen in a friendly and positive way. Dave has found me talking to women at Parkrun, at the supermarket or running club. In Harwich, I work with a local group that we set up known as the Harwich Hot Flushes which helps offer menopause and women's health education to the community.

Moving Forward, I Still Hate March

It has taken me many months to write what you are now reading, partly because like many others, I am juggling the commitments of full-time work, study and normal life, and also because it wasn't always an easy journey to write about. It triggered a lot of thoughts I had hidden away in the so-called cupboard in my brain and I wasn't always keen to open the door again. I would often write in short stints churning out a particular subject or saying to myself to aim 500 words per day. There would also be gaps in the writing process when other things had to take priority such as the day job lecturing or my PhD work.

But I kept chipping away, and I would often make notes on my phone during the work commute of ideas. I wanted to write about or look into further, and over time, words started to appear on paper or should I say screen and things started to take shape. As I currently type, it's March 2024. I've been feeling a little out of sorts, a bit low in my mood and easily triggered and it hit me as it's March, this was the month I was at my sickest and when I had the miscarriage. March was the month when I realised it was all over for us. March was the month when I it was the end of our fertility journey. March was the month when I lost our baby. It's 2024, I hear you say, it's been 7 years since it happened, and you still feel it? Pangs of grief, triggers or thoughts on what should have been. Grief is definitely like waves on a beach; some days, the waves are flat and you feel at home on the beach having a paddle. Other days, the waves are coming in thick and fast and it's not a day you want to paddle. It just seems that the waves are always felt more at certain times of the year for my own feelings.

It's important to remember that everyone experiences grief and loss differently and there is no right or wrong. It's about recognising and acknowledging the grief and seeking out support when you need it. Support looks so different for all of us, it could be counselling, a support group, talking to a friend, or like me having cuddles with one of your furry friends. Grief is a personal experience with no two of us going through the same journey. Some years are easier than others but March for me is a month I tend to remember and look back. I often pause and remember what could have been and think about what life would have looked like. I also try to remind myself of the new path and the things that matter on this path.

Fertility Fact

Why Do We Need More Research on Women's Health?

For far too long, women's health has been under-researched and underfunded. Women make up half of the population and a growing proportion of the workforce. At present, the current healthcare system was built by men for men and is failing women. Women were excluded from drug trials until the early 1990s as it was thought that hormonal fluctuations due to the menstrual cycle would complicate any data analysis. Researchers also concerned that there could be an impact on reproductive age females and their fertility. Whilst this was a generous gesture, it led to neglecting women in medical research for many years. This created a vacuum of data and outcomes that still impact us today. The under-representation of women in medical research has meant that women's diseases may be missed, mis-diagnosed or remain a mystery. This meant that health research has heavily focused on men with the results then applied to women under the assumption that the female body would react to drugs and other therapies in the same way as a man's body.

Historically, large funding bodies have not favoured women's health and reproductive research with a lot of funding going to conditions that impacted both men and women. There is also a lack of knowledge regarding conditions that affect women such as endometriosis, which is just as common as diabetes. If we compare the amount of research and specialised care available for diabetes, this wins hands down compared to what is out there for endometriosis research and care. There remains a sizable gap in the understanding of what we know about the female body.

Until more research is done on women's health, women will continue to be ignored and dismissed when they speak to their healthcare professional about their condition or symptoms. Whilst things are starting to change, there is still taboo around women's health issues. By elevating the importance of women's health, we can deliver better care and have more inclusive data and accessible solutions to help women across the globe. The good news is that there has been a shift in attitudes and this positive change has helped influence more women taking part in medical research.

Chapter 15

How Has the Journey Shaped My Nursing Practice?

One of the things I am often asked is about how my journey has impacted or changed my practice as a nurse and researcher working in the same area. The truth is that this was a unique challenge both at the time of the journey and once the journey had ended. I am also asked if I told my patients about my journey. In truth, I would only tell my patients if they asked as I didn't want it to be all about me and my journey, when seeing patients, it is all about them and their journey. My role is to educate and support them on their journey whatever that journey looks or feels like. Usually, most of my patients are understandably focused on their journey during clinics and consultations. Strange as it sounds, I rehearsed a short paragraph in my mind so that when the few that did ask, I would have something to tell them in a short professional way. I didn't want to not tell the truth, but equally, I didn't want to become emotional or make the patient feel uncomfortable. Over time, I have a little paragraph in my mind, a summary answer of our journey in brief that gives an honest answer to patients that take time to ask.

Being open and honest in navigating our journey has had an impact on my practice as a nurse and researcher in the area where I was also a patient. Although not all my patients know it, going through a similar journey with them means that I have also experienced something similar to them. I have sat in the same chair or couch that they have and experienced the same highs and lows after a scan. I have sat in the recovery room and listened to the magic egg number after an egg collection and held my breath twice for the day after a call from the embryologists telling me how many eggs have fertilised and become embryos. During two embryo transfers, I have counted to fifty in my head to take my mind off, having a full bladder and stared at the screen on the scanner, looking for the little flash telling us the embryo has travelled in the air or fluid into the right place in the endometrial cavity. I have also survived two, two-week waits, the desperate temptation not to test early, and the joys of using vaginal progesterone pessaries. I have also grieved silently when the test was negative and when the scan showed that our pregnancy wasn't viable. It's like wearing different shoes but walking the same paths; some things are the same and some things are different.

The journey gives me a unique experience as a nurse and as a patient, understanding the journey from both sides, the professional as well as the patient, which provides a unique understanding and support to the patients I care for. Not just being aware of the medical aspects, results, medication and terminology but also the human aspect, how it felt to have an ultrasound scan, egg collection and embryo transfer, how it feels to take medication and how it feels to experience the highs and lows of the fertility journey rollercoaster.

Epilogue

Our infertility journey began in 2013 and ended in 2018 when we decided to donate our remaining embryo to research. We both, over time, have learnt to live on a new path and moved forward. As I type in the summer of 2023, I am still teaching women's health, working independently and studying for my PhD. Dave and I are still together with our four dogs known as the Pleace Pack and he is still working in his manufacturing technician job. If there is one thing that the journey has taught us, it is to take time to value the simple things in life that often mean the most, a walk with the dogs, a chat with friends or enjoying a good piece of cake.

Healthwise at the moment, I have a good HRT regime which includes the Mirena coil as this offers the lowest localised amount of progesterone, oestrogel – a gel that contains oestrogen – and medication that keeps symptoms relatively stable, and I don't currently see any specialists. I have had some lasting effects that required intervention, this was paid for privately by myself and my mum. It included vaginal surgery to remove some of the damaged skin on my labia from the genital swelling and recent eye surgery for bilateral cataracts; however, the doctors are unsure if this is connected to any of the hormone issues I have experienced but is extremely unusual because I was only in my late 30s when I had the surgery which is a young age to develop cataracts.

It would be wrong to say that we are over it, I don't think

that it is something you can ever get over and for us, we just learnt to move forward. Like many others who have suffered grief, time is a great healer and you also learn to grow with it and around it. We both deal with it in different ways, some days are better than others. Initially, walking a new path was hard, but now, we are stronger and have learnt to accept the path we walk. Not a day goes by where I don't think about what had happened or what could have been, but over time that voice is a little quieter. I still take time to remember the baby loss week and will often feel uneasy during March, looking back, that was the time I went for the pregnancy scan. I also have a beautiful painting of our embryo in a frame on my desk in my home office. Those who might have had a consultation with me or a Zoom call would have likely seen the flash of blue on their camera.

The journey has changed me, I am not the same person I was before our fertility journey started, and the journey has changed some of my friendships and how others see me. I have a great group of core friends from school, my work family, running and other parts of my life, you know who you are. My family remains an integral source of support. But over time, I feel I have also grown as a person, I am now not afraid to try things I might not have done before such as pushing myself into studying, setting up a support group or running a marathon. This can only be a good thing and over time slowly but surely, I felt brave enough to share my story so that it could help others. Whilst I have never met anyone else with a similar experience, if by reading this book it helps just one person, then my work is done.

If you are reading this and worried, maybe you first understand that a journey like mine with this condition is incredibly rare and if you have concerns, please reach out to your doctor or fertility specialist. Also, know that everyone responds differently to hormones and medication and no journey is unique. Information and research are always changing, so what might have been written about now may not be the same in the future. That is the beauty of always campaigning for more research in women's health. With more research, we are likely to find out more information and possible future treatment options. Finally, don't be afraid to share your story, your story is unique and powerful and may help others.

References

Allbright, F, Smith, P, H, Fraser, R, (1942) *A Syndrome Characterised by Primary Ovarian Insufficiency and Decreased Stature: Report of 11 Cases with a Digression in Hormonal Control of Axillary and Pubic Hair*; American Journal of Medical Science 204 Pg 625–648.

Bernstein, J, Patel D, Fine, L. (2022) *A focused Report on Progesterone Hypersensitivity*; Expert Review of Clinical Immunology.

Chiarella, S, Bucheit, K, Foer, D. (2023) *Progesterone Hypersensitivity*; The Journal of Allergy and Clinical Immunology: In Practice 11(12). P3606–3613.

Di Renzo, C, Tosto, V, Tsibizova, V. (2020) *Progesterone: History, Facts and Artifacts*; Best Practice and Research Clinical Obstetrics and Gynaecology 1(69). Pg 2–12.

Foer, D, Buchheit, K. (2019) *Presentation and Natural History of Progesterone Hypersensitivity*; *Annals of Allergy, Asthma and Immunology*; 122(2) The Journal of Allergy and Clinical Immunology 6(4).

Itskeson, A, Seidman, D, Zolti, M, Carp, A. (2011) *Steroid Hormone Hypersensitivity: Clinical Presentation and Management*; Journal of Fertility and Sterility.

Kuruvilla, M, Vanjicharoenkarn, K, Wan, J, Pereira, N, Chung, P. (2018) *Exogenous Progesterone Hypersensitivity Associated with Recurrent Pregnancy Loss.*

Nelson, L, (2009) *Primary Ovarian Insufficiency*; New England Journal of Medicine; 360 Pg 606–614.

Nguyen, T, Ahmed, A. (2016) *Autoimmune Progesterone Dermatitis: Update and Insights*; Autoimmunity Reviews 15(2).

Patel, D, Fine, L, Bernstein, J. (2023) *A focused Report on Progesterone Hypersensitivity*; Expert Review of Clinical Immunology; (19)4.

Piette, P. (2018) *The History of Natural Progesterone, the Never-ending Story*; Climacteric Sundstrom-Poromaa, I, Comasco, E, Sumner, R, Luders, E. (2020) Progesterone – Friend or foe? Frontiers in Neuroendocrinology 1(59).

Useful Resources

Podcasts
The Fertility Podcast
Life and Soul Podcast

Books
The Complete Guide to POI and Early Menopause by Dr Hannah Short and Dr Mandy Leonhardt
My Life on Pause by Dr Siobhan O'Sullivan
Life Almost by Jennie Agg
Saying Goodbye by Zoe Clark-Coates
The Baby Loss Guide by Zoe Clark-Coates
The Worst Girl Gang Ever by Bex Gunn and Laura Buckingham
Living the Life Unexpected by Jodie Day
The Pursuit of Motherhood by Jessica Hepburn
Womb by Leah Hazard
The XX Brain by Lisa Mosconi

Support Groups
Whilst there is no specific support group for progesterone hypersensitivity, there are a number of support groups that might be helpful for some of the issues highlighted in this book:
The Miscarriage Association
Tommy's
Cradle
Saying goodbye

Fertility Network
Donor Conception Network
Menopause Support
The Daisy Network
British Infertility Counselling
The Dovecoate
Gateway Women

Guidelines and Reviews

NICE Menopause Guidelines
NICE Fertility Guidelines
ESHRE POI Guidelines
The Independent Pregnancy Loss Review

Author's Notes

If you would like to get in touch, you can follow me on the following social media accounts:

Instagram – @fertility_menopause_support

Twitter – @katepleacewww.fertilitymenopausesupport.com

My PhD Ongoing Work:

The Centre for Reproduction Research De Montfort University

https://www.dmu.ac.uk/research/centres-institutes/crr/index.aspx#:~:text=The%20Centre%20for%20Reproduction%20Research,of%20disciplines%2C%20approaches%20and%20methods